Leaves of Prayer

ST. JOHN THE EVANGELIST CHURCH
SPENCERPORT, NY 14559

Leaves of Prayer

✦

Scriptural Passages and Catholic Reflections For Those Who Enjoy Nature

Anthony R. Brach

To Marcia + Jack
with Love
Mother + Dad
aug 2002

Writers Club Press

San Jose New York Lincoln Shanghai

Leaves of Prayer
Scriptural Passages and Catholic Reflections For Those Who Enjoy Nature

Writers Club Press
an imprint of iUniverse, Inc.

For information address:
iUniverse, Inc.
5220 S. 16th St., Suite 200
Lincoln, NE 68512
www.iuniverse.com

ISBN: 0-595-23707-X

Printed in the United States of America

I dedicate this book to my family, my wife Ying and our children Jonathan, Richard, and Joseph, my parents and brothers, relatives, and friends with whom I've celebrated God's creation, love, and mercy outdoors, at home, and in Church.

Question the beauty of the earth. Question the beauty of the sea...question the beauty of the sky...All respond, "See, we are beautiful." Their beauty is a profession. These beauties are subject to change. Who made them if not the Beautiful One who is not subject to change?
—St. Augustine (354–430, *Sermon* 241, 2).

Contents

List of Illustrations xi

Foreword xv

Preface xvii

CHAPTER 1   Introduction 1

CHAPTER 2   Creation 5

CHAPTER 3   The Universe and The Sun 17

CHAPTER 4   The Rainbow and The Aurora. 23

CHAPTER 5   Seasons 27

CHAPTER 6   Earth. 35

CHAPTER 7   Mountains and Hills 49

CHAPTER 8   The Rock 57

CHAPTER 9   Wind. 69

CHAPTER 10   Water 75

CHAPTER 11   Ice and Snow. 83

CHAPTER 12   Lightning and Fire. 87

CHAPTER 13   Flora 95

CHAPTER 14   Fauna 107

CHAPTER 15   Wings and Angels 113

CHAPTER 16   The Human Family. 123

CHAPTER 17 Servants and Co-Creators 133

CHAPTER 18 Suffering 143

CHAPTER 19 Death and Resurrection 151

CHAPTER 20 Conclusion 157

About the Author 171

References 173

List of Illustrations

Chapter 1, fig. 1. *Christ in the form of the fish, representing the Trinity.*

Chapter 2, fig. 1. *Tau Cross with alpha and omega.*

Chapter 3, fig. 1. *The Nativity.*

Chapter 4, fig. 1. *Noah's Ark.*

Chapter 5, fig. 1. *Dicentra eximia* (Ker Gawl.) Torr.—flowers of wild bleeding heart.

Chapter 6, fig. 1. *The Divine Meal.*

Chapter 7, fig. 1. Glacier National Park, British Columbia.

Chapter 8, fig. 1. Chimney Bluffs on Lake Ontario, New York.

Chapter 9, fig. 1. A seagull.

Chapter 10, fig. 1. Blackwater Falls State Park, West Virginia.

Chapter 11, fig. 1. Snowman and children.

Chapter 12, fig. 1. *The Burning Bush.*

Chapter 13, fig. 1. The Lily. The symbol of the Virgin Mary.

    fig. 2. Pressed flower of *Anemone coronaria* L. from the Holy Land.

Chapter 14, fig. 1. A seahorse.

Chapter 15, fig. 1. A dove.

Chapter 16, fig. 1. *"I am the Vine, ye are the branches."*

  fig. 2. The author's family.

Chapter 17, fig. 1. *The Washing of Feet.*

  fig. 2. *Archangel Raphael.*

Chapter 18, fig. 1. *The Crown of Thorns.*

  fig. 2. Pressed thistle plant *Gundelia tournefortii* L.

Chapter 19, fig. 1. *The Butterfly, a symbol of the Resurrection of the Body.*

  fig. 2. Image of the Face on the Shroud with 3-D enhancement.

Chapter 20, fig. 1. *The Triumphant Lamb, after the Revelation of John.*

Acknowledgments

I thank my parents who taught me to treasure God's gifts of the natural world and the Church—the Word and the Sacraments, my wife for encouraging me to write, and my children for their continual questions and sense of wonder about the earth and life. I thank my cousin Walter Macior (Father Lazarus) for writing the foreword and for his helpful comments, and my Mom for reading an early draft. I am grateful to my brother Paul Gerard for his generous help with the images, and thanks to him and my father Paul Joseph for sharing their photos.

Scripture taken from the *Good News Bible in Today's English Version—Second Edition*, Copyright © 1992 by American Bible Society; and from the *New International Version* (denoted in text by acronym NIV). Used by Permission. Excerpts from the English translation of the *Catechism of the Catholic Church* for use in the United States of America Copyright 1994, United States Catholic Conference, Inc.—Libreria Editrice Vaticana. Used with Permission.

I am thankful for permission from the Vatican Information Service to include quotations from the Holy Father, Br. Paschal of Marytown to include quotes from St. Maximilian Kolbe, Steve Shawl to include the August 1999 message and Father Slavko Barbaric's reflection from Medjugorje, and Professor Gerhard P. Knapp to include the *Romulus the Great* quotation, and the *Saturday Evening Post* Society to include the quote from Marc Chagall. Sources for quotations are duly noted throughout.

I am grateful to Alan D. Whanger, MD, for sharing the photograph of the Face on the Shroud and permitting its use. Thanks to Arion Press for courtesy of use of *Christian symbols* drawn by Rudolf Koch with the collaboration of Fritz Kredel, to the National Oceanic and Atmospheric Administration (NOAA)/Department of Commerce for courtesy of use of images, and to the staff of the Harvard University Herbaria for use of collections. I thank the publisher iUniverse for assistance with cover and book design.

Foreword

In a world beset, for the first time, with the very real prospect of anni-
hilation of the human race, this broad spectrum collection of quotations from the Bible and other sources, together with the author's
reflections comes like a refreshing spring rain on a parched earth.

The passages are organized in 20 chapters mostly according to such
natural history topics as flora, fauna, the earth, the universe, the seasons, but with others identified with creation, co-creation, angels, suffering and death. The integration of the secular (the natural) with the
spiritual (the supernatural) by the author is a novel approach much
needed in a world where these two viewpoints are often aggressively
and confusedly pitted against each other.

Quotations of Henry David Thoreau (from a secular standpoint)
echo the sacred expressions of St. Francis of Assisi, both extolling the
beauty of Nature but from different perspectives. By judicious selection, the author has created a *vade mecum* to accompany the Nature-
loving naturalist on a stroll through a meadow or forest pausing now
and again to read a line or two and ponder more deeply the meaning of
it all.

It also serves as a mini-concordance of both sacred and secular sub-
jects for those whose memory is as weak as their faith is strong. Tucked
in among many pages of biblical reference one will find quotations of
Plato, St. Augustine, Mark Twain, St. Maximilian Kolbe, Pascal, Pope
John Paul II, and many other serious thinkers. (The "Catholic" in the
title refers to Anthony Brach's reflections and not necessarily to the
religious affiliation of all the contributors.) The book is for all readers.
A short meditation accompanies each chapter.

The book is written "...for those who enjoy Nature", and the
author suggests that scientists, of which he is one, have searched for

God through evolutionary theory and "deep ecology." Those Catholics and others, who believe that an understanding of natural evolutionary theory is incompatible with a belief in a supernatural Creator, fail to distinguish the natural from the supernatural and deify the earth as "Gaia" and "Mother Nature." Creation is a supernatural act making something from absolutely nothing. Evolution is the sequence of change between living beings through time (i.e., "descent with modification"). *Leaves of Prayer* is a collage of spiritual readings and not a theological treatise nor a scientific report. It invites the reader to come aside a while, reflect on the meaning of Creation and enjoy the peace and quiet of deep meditation. For those of us scientists who have done so, Darwin rings true: "The birth both of the species and of the individual are equally parts of that grand sequence of events which our minds refuse to accept as the result of blind chance." Evolution *does* involve chance and natural selection, but for humans it involves much more. Understanding is followed by appreciation and only humans can appreciate the "grand sequence of events" that Nature provides. Finally, appreciation leads to love for the Creator, which was expressed so eloquently yet so simply by St. Francis of Assisi's characterizing non-human creatures as his brothers and sisters! *Leaves of Prayer* is a step in that direction.

Lazarus Walter Macior, O.F.M.
Professor of Biology, Emeritus
13 June 2002 (Feast of St. Anthony of Padua)

Preface

Each of us has our own experiences of life and the natural world, which lead us to ponder the Mystery of God's creation. Within these pages (or *Leaves*), I compiled my favorite Biblical passages, quotations, and reflections for prayer, study, and meditation. I hope you enjoy the beauty of the individual *Leaves* as well as the entire tree. I arranged this short book from a Christian viewpoint, as a Roman Catholic, who appreciates both the natural world and human life. I ask God to bless you, the reader, that you may grow closer to the Creator and to a greater awareness of our role to protect life as helpful servants of our brothers and sisters, and wise and holy managers of the earth and its resources.

In addition to the treasure of the Word contained in Holy Scripture and the Real Presence of Jesus in the Blessed Sacrament, there are countless possible moments in our lives and the environment speaking volumes about God. In my own life, my parents were my first teachers directing me to signs of God's Love and Presence. They were faithful in bringing my brothers and me to Church, praying at home, taking us on walks and family trips to parks, mountains, lakes, forests, and Shrines, teaching us how to swim, guiding us through school, homework and activities, scouting, camping, hiking, backpacking, canoeing, and star-gazing, and onto college and careers. We planted vegetables and flowers, watered plants and weeded, played and swam, raked leaves, and shovelled snow. We filled bird feeders at the nature sanctuary, watched nuthatches, chickadees, and woodpeckers. We walked through bogs and woods, and helped on trail days. We botanized and learned the names of plants. We watched sunrises, sunsets, and eclipses of the moon. We enjoyed time together visiting relatives and friends.

Upon receiving the Sacrament of Confirmation, I chose St. Francis of Assisi as a patron saint since he was close to God and all His creatures "great and small." While on camp staff in the Adirondack Mountains (1981), I was inspired by remarkable sunrises, sudden thunderstorms, the flora and fauna, and night constellations. In college (1981–1986), particular Scriptural passages became appealing and the focus of meditations, especially during the *Liturgy of the Hours*. In graduate school (1987–1993), my wife and I enjoyed exploring nearby parks. I started editing for an international botanical project (1993). Our family begins Sunday at Mass at our parish Church, and then we take the family on day trips much like my parents did for us.

I was touched by the words of Pope John Paul II on a human ecology, and a meditation by Father Barbaric of Medjugorje, and I very much wanted to share these. Thanks to the Mary Foundation, St. Jude Media, and Marytown, I was inspired by the writings of St. Maximilian Kolbe and my family enrolled as Knights of Immaculata in 1997, and soon after, I learned about current research findings on the Shroud of Turin connected with botany. All of these various happenings and the wish to share the Gospel's profound message of life, faith, and hope with my children and the interested reader have contributed to the organization for this book.

The title *Leaves of Prayer* presents multiple meanings. First, I arranged the book as a book of prayer and meditation. Pages of books have sometimes been referred to as "leaves", and reasonably so when we recall the origin of the paper. Secondly, each Scriptural passage and quotation is like a leaf arranged on a tree. Thirdly, the photos and drawings provide wonderful leaves upon which to reflect. As the saying goes, "a picture is worth a thousand words." Fourthly, when joined or uplifted, our hands can be thought of as "leaves of prayer." Finally, we are branches on the Vine Who is Jesus, together forming the Church, the Body of Christ, the Kingdom of God.

1

Introduction

Christ in the form of the fish, representing the Trinity.
Drawn by Rudolf Koch. Courtesy of Arion Press.

*****

Have you ever been amazed by the wonders of the earth, life, and the universe? Every day, there is something new, something remarkable that awes us. We are reminded of our smallness in relation to the vast expanse of the universe. There is an amazing intricacy in the details of structure and function. It is fascinating how all the systems of life and nature are designed to work together. From sunrise to sunset, dew and rain, ice and snow, sunshine and clouds, rainbows and auroras, flowers and bird songs, babies to the elderly, smiling faces and helping hands, we are moved to praise and thank God our Creator.

Throughout history, humankind has variously responded to God our Creator. Scientists have searched for answers through evolutionary theory, metaphysics, and "deep ecology." People of various religions have sought truths about creation and life. Sometimes, people confused and misidentified nature, the earth, and creatures themselves as "gods."

When persons find God, they find the source of all truth, all that is good, beautiful, unifying, and holy. Today as we are in sorrow at the tragedies of life and the world, we realize that every one of us is called to holiness, to live in accord with our families, communities, and creation around us. We live holy lives when we radiate the love and peace of God, and when we offer Him our hearts, hands, minds, and strength to share in His work of creation. The opposite of God's Goodness and Life is evil; in fact, it is literally the opposite spelling of the word "*Live*." We are called to plant and to restore, to nurture life, not to destroy.

To save all humankind from all that which is not life giving, God inspired the authors of Holy Scripture, i.e., the *Holy Bible*—The Word of God, to tell us about their experiences leading them to the Loving God whom called them. They were Israelites, the Hebrews, the Jews, and the first Christians. They told us about God and life from their perspectives and experiences living close to the land and sea as shepherds, farmers, and fishermen. For us as Christians, we believe that God sent us His only Son, Jesus, the Word made flesh, the Way, the Truth, and the Life. We listen to Him Who is the Word Himself when we read the Holy Bible and hear the Word proclaimed.

Our reflecting upon Biblical passages directs us to our Triune God, one God in three Persons, the Mystery beautifully reflected in the form of the shamrock by St. Patrick. The first leaflet reminds us of the first Person of this Trinity, the Providential Father and Creator. The second leaflet reminds us of the second Person, Jesus Son of God and Son of Man, the new Adam, the Living Word Himself. Finally, the third leaflet reminds us of the third Person, the Holy Spirit, the Love between the Father and the Son, Who renews the Life of God within us and in the Church. Together the three leaflets are one leaf. We pray to the Father, through our Lord Jesus, in union with the Holy Spirit. We are changed and renewed by God's new creation through the Resurrection of Jesus.

May God bless us and guide us on our continuing lifelong journey to Him. The pilgrimage begins from a tiny seed (our conception), to germination (our birth), to growth as a seedling (our childhood and youth), to growth into a mature tree (our adulthood), and finally to death (and Heaven, if we choose God's Way of Life, thanks be to God). May we be firmly rooted in faith and the life of the Church, the Word and the Sacraments. May we grow with the Light of Christ and together form that perfect tree, the living vine, the Kingdom of God.

May the Mother of Jesus, the Mother given to us at the "tree" of the Cross, shower us with healing and life-giving graces from God. She replaces Eve as the mother of all the living. Because she is the spouse of the Holy Spirit, Mary is a wonderful advocate. She and all the saints were responsible stewards of life. The angels, too, treasure life; they sang at the birth of the Christ Child, cried at the death of our Savior, and rejoiced at the Resurrection. May all the saints and angels guide all of us to Jesus, the Light of the World, the Living Water, and the Bread of Life. May the words of Holy Scripture and the images of God's creation remind us that we are all created in God's image and are called to live united as the human family, as God's children, in justice and peace as brothers and sisters.

Selected Scriptural passages are grouped into topics or themes associated with God's creation and life. It is best to reflect upon Holy Scripture within the proper context of associated verses, Biblical themes, historical events, and their meaning for us today. Following selected verses, I have quoted from Catholic Saints and scholars of various faiths to reflect upon the Mystery of God's creation and our role as servants of one another, and caretakers of life and the environment. We would do well to reflect upon their encouraging thoughts. May God inspire us to share our faith as well.

*****

And the philosopher, always holding converse through reason with the idea of being, is also dark from excess of light; for the souls of the many have no eye which can endure the vision of the divine.
—Plato (428–348 BC), *The Sophist.*

*****

Nature has some perfections, to show that she is the image of God; and some defects, to show that she is only His image.
—Blaise Pascal (1623–1662). Pensées [1670], Sect. VIII.

*****

Life is motion, a tending toward a purpose.
—St. Maximilian Kolbe (1894–1941). *Aim Higher!: Spiritual and Marian reflections of St. Maximilian Kolbe.* Prow Books / Franciscan Marytown Press.

2

Creation

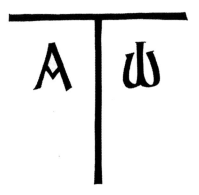

Tau Cross with alpha and omega.
Drawn by Rudolf Koch. Courtesy of Arion Press.

*****

As every story and every life has its beginning, so too there is the very Beginning to all creation. As we look up at the stars, comets and meteorites, the planets and the moon, and around at the earth, oceans and lakes, deserts and swamps, mountains and hills, the flora and fauna, and the peoples around us, we reflect upon the work of the Divine Architect. St. Thomas Aquinas referred to God the Creator as the "Unmoved Mover." God, Who Himself is Eternal, created out of nothing. He initiated the universe and life itself. God directed and continues to guide evolution and humankind in this great journey, this pilgrimage of life. May we be faithful pilgrims on this wonderful voyage of life. May we be responsible creatures and co-creators.

5

*****

Genesis Chapter 1
The Story of Creation
In the beginning God created the heavens and the earth. The earth was barren, with no form of life; it was under a roaring ocean covered with darkness. But the Spirit of God was moving over the water.

The First Day
God said, "I command light to shine!" And light started shining. God looked at the light and saw that it was good. He separated light from darkness and named the light "Day" and the darkness "Night." Evening came and then morning—that was the first day.

The Second Day
God said, "I command a dome to separate the water above it from the water below it." And that's what happened. God made the dome and named it "Sky." Evening came and then morning—that was the second day.

The Third Day
God said, "I command the water under the sky to come together in one place, so there will be dry ground." And that's what happened. God named the dry ground "Land," and he named the water "Ocean." God looked at what he had done and saw that it was good. God said, "I command the earth to produce all kinds of plants, including fruit trees and grain." And that's what happened. The earth produced all kinds of vegetation. God looked at what he had done, and it was good. Evening came and then morning—that was the third day.

The Fourth Day
God said, "I command lights to appear in the sky and to separate day from night and to show the time for seasons, special days, and years. I command them to shine on the earth." And that's what happened. God made two powerful lights, the brighter one to rule the day and the other to rule the night. He also made the stars. Then God put these lights in the sky to shine on the earth, to rule day and night, and to separate light from darkness. God looked at what he had done, and it was good. Evening came and then morning—that was the fourth day.

The Fifth Day

God said, "I command the ocean to be full of living creatures, and I command birds to fly above the earth." So God made the giant sea monsters and all the living creatures that swim in the ocean. He also made every kind of bird. God looked at what he had done, and it was good. Then he gave the living creatures his blessing—he told the ocean creatures to live everywhere in the ocean and the birds to live everywhere on earth. Evening came and then morning—that was the fifth day.

The Sixth Day

God said, "I command the earth to give life to all kinds of tame animals, wild animals, and reptiles." And that's what happened. God made every one of them. Then he looked at what he had done, and it was good. God said, "Now we will make humans, and they will be like us. We will let them rule the fish, the birds, and all other living creatures." So God created humans to be like himself; he made men and women. God gave them his blessing and said: Have a lot of children! Fill the earth with people and bring it under your control. Rule over the fish in the ocean, the birds in the sky, and every animal on the earth. I have provided all kinds of fruit and grain for you to eat. And I have given the green plants as food for everything else that breathes. These will be food for animals, both wild and tame, and for birds. God looked at what he had done. All of it was very good! Evening came and then morning—that was the sixth day.

*****

And God saw that it was good. Creation is beautiful yet subject to the Creator of all. "How wonderful is Your Name O Lord, Our God!" (Psalm 75:1). The stars and planets, creatures of every kind, birds and fish, flowers and trees, and we Your children proclaim Your majesty. May we have eyes to see the goodness and beauty in each created thing and in every human person. May we respect God's Ways and be responsible servants of one another, and caretakers of the gifts and resources entrusted to us. May we give out of genuine concern for those who share this planet Earth with us. May we be wise in our utilization of this world's goods so as to provide for present and future generations.

*****

Genesis 2
So the heavens and the earth and everything else were created.
The Seventh Day
By the seventh day God had finished his work, and so he rested. God blessed the seventh day and made it special because on that day he rested from his work. That's how God created the heavens and the earth. When the LORD God made the heavens and the earth,
The Garden of Eden
no grass or plants were growing anywhere. God had not yet sent any rain, and there was no one to work the land. But streams came up from the ground and watered the earth. The LORD God took a handful of soil and made a man. God breathed life into the man, and the man started breathing. The LORD made a garden in a place called Eden, which was in the east, and he put the man there. The LORD God placed all kinds of beautiful trees and fruit trees in the garden. Two other trees were in the middle of the garden. One of the trees gave life—the other gave the power to know the difference between right and wrong. From Eden a river flowed out to water the garden, then it divided into four rivers. The first one is the Pishon River that flows through the land of Havilah, where pure gold, rare perfumes, and precious stones are found. The second is the Gihon River that winds through Ethiopia. The Tigris River that flows east of Assyria is the third, and the fourth is the Euphrates River. The LORD God put the man in the Garden of Eden to take care of it and to look after it. But the LORD told him, "You may eat fruit from any tree in the garden, except the one that has the power to let you know the difference between right and wrong. If you eat any fruit from that tree, you will die before the day is over!" The LORD God said, "It isn't good for the man to live alone. I need to make a suitable partner for him." So the LORD took some soil and made animals and birds. He brought them to the man to see what names he would give each of them.

Then the man named the tame animals and the birds and the wild animals. That's how they got their names. None of these was the right kind of partner for the man. So the LORD God made him fall into a deep sleep, and he took out one of the man's ribs. Then after closing the man's side, the LORD made a woman out of the rib. The LORD God brought her to the man, and the man exclaimed, "Here is someone like me! She is part of my body, my own flesh and bones. She came from me, a man. So I will name her Woman!" That's why a man will leave his own father and mother. He marries a woman, and the two of them become like one person. Although the man and his wife were both naked, they were not ashamed.

*****

The second account of Creation is another beautiful reflection upon God's Goodness. God formed man from the dust of the ground and gave him the breath of life. Man's seemingly simple act of naming the other creatures reminds us of our role to be care-givers and stewards of one another and all the flora and fauna surrounding us. In this story, God formed woman from one of man's ribs. How perfect the combination of man and woman, husband and wife, that they compliment each other and become one. May God bless marriages and families with unity and love.

The following chapter of Genesis tells us the story of the fall of our first parents. God gave them free will upon their creation in the Garden of Eden, a garden of paradise. In the center of the garden were both the tree of life and the tree of knowledge of good and evil. Adam and Eve could have been very happy with the rest of the trees including the tree of life. However, they did not listen to God—they disobeyed His command. They did not choose the tree of life but instead ate the fruit of the tree of knowledge of good and evil. They sinned in their pride and disobedience. Original sin, disorder, and strife entered the world. Adam and Eve were banished from the garden and all seemed lost. However, God in His Goodness, had a plan to save all humankind. From Noah, to Abraham, the kings and prophets, we read the record of salvation history. Finally, God sent forth His own Son born of a woman. Jesus, Son of God and Son of Man, suffered, died, and rose to forgive our sins. Thus, He restored order to creation and saved humankind, offering us again the "tree of life" (Rev 22:14).

The fact that there are two accounts of creation reminds us that God created all things, directed, and guides creation's evolution, even now. There is no conflict between religion and science. Instead may we always have a place for both faith and reason. May God grant us renewed faith (courage, strength, piety, fear of the Lord) to sustain our relationships to God and one another. May God bless us with reason (knowledge, understanding, counsel) to help solve the world's problems and to develop answers with respect for one another and for the earth and its creatures.

*****

Psalm 148
Come Praise the LORD
Shout praises to the LORD!
Shout the LORD's praises
in the highest heavens.
All of you angels,
and all who serve him above,
come and offer praise.
Sun and moon,
and all of you bright stars,
come and offer praise.
Highest heavens,
and the water
above the highest heavens,
come and offer praise.
Let all things praise
the name of the LORD,
because they were created
at his command.
He made them to last forever,
and nothing can change

what he has done.
All creatures on earth,
you obey his commands,
so come praise the LORD!
Sea monsters and the deep sea,
fire and hail,
snow and frost,
and every stormy wind,
come praise the LORD!
All mountains and hills,
fruit trees and cedars,
every wild and tame animal,
all reptiles and birds,
come praise the LORD!
Every king and every ruler,
all nations on earth,
every man and every woman,
young people and old,
come praise the LORD!
All creation, come praise
the name of the LORD.
Praise his name alone.
The glory of God is greater
than heaven and earth.
Like a bull with mighty horns,
the LORD protects
his faithful nation Israel,
because they belong to him.
Shout praises to the LORD!

*****

Every artistic work credits the artist. Prayer can inspire and energize the artist. In turn, reflecting upon the art can become a prayer. May we take time to reflect upon inspired, sacred art, icons as windows to the divine, statues and pictures of saints, holy men and women, poetry and meditations, and the Holy Bible. Together with all creation in adoration before the Blessed Sacrament, we worship and praise God, the Divine Artist and Craftsman, who made us and provides for us.

*****

Hail, holy light! Offspring of heav'n firstborn.
—John Milton (1608–1674). *Paradise Lost* [1667].

*****

The year's at the spring
And day's at the morn;
Morning's at seven;
The hillside's dew-pearled;
The lark's on the wing;
The snail's on the thorn;
God's in his heaven—
All's right with the world!
—Robert Browning (1812–1889). *Pippa Passes* [1841], pt. 1, *"Morning."*

*****

Our Father in heaven is the first beginning and final end of everything...From the Father through the Son and Spirit descends each act of the love of God, creating, sustaining in existence, giving life and its development both in the order of nature as well as in the order of grace....With God everything, without God nothing!...God wants to draw the soul to himself through love.
—St. Maximilian Kolbe. *Aim Higher!: Spiritual and Marian reflections of St. Maximilian Kolbe.* Prow Books / Franciscan Marytown Press. With permission.

*****

As I make my way across Poland, I contemplate the beauty of this, my native country and I am reminded of this particular aspect of the saving mission of the Son of God. Here, the blue of the sky, the green of the woods and fields, the silver of the lakes and rivers, all seem to speak with exceptional power. Here the song of the birds sounds so very familiar, so Polish. All of this testifies to the love of the Creator.

—Pope John Paul II, 12 June 1999 (VIS—Vatican Information Service). With permission.

*****

The glory of the Trinity shines out in creation. In fact, it is possible to see, in the light of Revelation, how the creative act is associated with the 'Father of lights with whom there is no variation or shadow due to change'…in Holy Scripture, creation is often also linked to the divine Word which bursts forth and acts.… At other times, Scripture highlights the role of the Spirit of God in the creative act.…That same Spirit is symbolically represented in the breath of the mouth of God. Faced with the glory of the Trinity in creation, man must contemplate, sing out, rediscover his wonder.…For believers, contemplating creation also comprehends listening to a message, hearing a paradoxical and silent voice…nature is a gospel that speaks to us of God.…this capacity to contemplate and know, this discovery of a transcendental presence in creation, must also lead us to rediscover our fraternal relationship with the earth, to which we are bound from the moment of our creation.… If nature is not violated and humiliated, she will once more become the sister of man.

—Pope John Paul II, 26 January 2000 (VIS—Vatican Information Service). With permission.

*****

The *Catechism of the Catholic Church* teaches and reminds us of the *Ways of Coming to Know God*:

> When he listens to the message of creation and to the voice of conscience, man can arrive at certainty about the existence of God, the cause and the end of everything (46).
> Created in God's image and called to know and love him, the person who seeks God discovers certain ways of coming to know him

...These "ways" of approaching God from creation have a twofold point of departure: the physical world, and the human person. (31).

The world: starting from movement, becoming, contingency, and the world's order and beauty, one can come to a knowledge of God as the origin and the end of the universe...(32).

The human person: with his openness to truth and beauty, his sense of moral goodness, his freedom and the voice of his conscience, with his longings for the infinite and for happiness, man questions himself about God's existence. In all this he discerns signs of his spiritual soul. The soul, the "seed of eternity we bear in ourselves, irreducible to the merely material", can have its origin only in God. (33).

The world, and man, attest that they contain within themselves neither their first principle nor their final end, but rather that they participate in Being itself, which alone is without origin or end. Thus, in different ways, man can come to know that there exists a reality which is the first cause and final end of all things, a reality "that everyone calls God." (34).

Man's faculties make him capable of coming to a knowledge of the existence of a personal God. But for man to be able to enter into real intimacy with him, God willed both to reveal himself to man, and to give him the grace of being able to welcome this revelation in faith.(so) The proofs of God's existence, however, can predispose one to faith and help one to see that faith is not opposed to reason. (35).

Man is in search of God. In the act of creation, God calls every being from nothingness into existence. "Crowned with glory and honor," man is, after the angels, capable of acknowledging "how majestic is the name of the Lord in all the earth." Even after losing through his sin his likeness to God, man remains an image of his Creator, and retains the desire for the one who calls him into existence. All religions bear witness to men's essential search for God. (2566).

—Excerpts from the English translation of the *Catechism of the Catholic Church* for use in the United States of America Copyright 1994, United States Catholic Conference, Inc.—Libreria Editrice Vaticana. Used with Permission.

*****

**All of Creation praises You, O Lord
(an Adirondack summer afternoon)**
Chipmunks run about.
Robins, sparrows, chickadees call out to each other.
Red squirrels chase one another in play.
Osprey soar above the bay.

Winds come and go from the lake.
Thunder pounds in the west.
The sun plays peek-a-boo from behind the clouds.
Clouds cover the blue dome.

Ants, alone, wander about aimlessly.
Phoebes and woodpeckers make themselves known.
Porcupines rest under cover until night.
The loon laughs at all.

Grouse fly away with a hurried rush.
Bees pass flower to flower of the raspberry.
The Sun dries the soil.
Leaves shake with the breeze.

The thunder approaches.
The winds increase.
Birds fly low. Wildlife takes shelter.
Insects gather together; ants build up their entrances.

Then everything is quiet as the Storm arrives.
Water drops out of the masses of water vapor.
Dripping on everything, the plants rejoice.
The birds sing as they enjoy the show.

Chipmunks and squirrels have taken shelter.
The insects have hidden themselves beneath leaves.

Lightning flashes, thunder echoes, rain pours
From the dome above us.

The soil soaks up the water; the plants will be satisfied; the wildlife is
singing.
The wind howls; thunder follows the lightning.
After awhile, the storm subsides and
All is well and fine.
—Anthony R. Brach (1981).

*****

O God, our Father, we stand before You with praise for the wonders
of Your creation, and with thanksgiving for the gift of Your Love. We
open our whole hearts to You and to Your children, our brothers and
sisters in You. Brother Jesus, may we walk, study, work, and rest with
You as we meet each other along life's journey and in times of solitude.
May Your Holy Spirit renew us with love, joy, and peace. Bless our
work as co-creators with You, stewards and caretakers of the earth and
life. Amen.

*****

Glory be to the Father, and to the Son, and to the Holy Spirit, as it
was in the beginning, is now, and will be forever. Amen.
—Doxology. A well-known prayer.

3

The Universe and The Sun

The Nativity.
Drawn by Rudolf Koch. Courtesy of Arion Press.

*****

The grandness of the universe is only a minute reflection of the grandeur of God. The universe began about 12 billion years ago and could contain 3 thousand million billion stars. As Copernicus realized that the Sun was at the center and the planets revolved around it (*De Revolutionibus Orbium Coelestium*), may we place God at the center of our hearts and our lives. May the heavenly lights lift our eyes, hearts, minds, and souls to God and remind us of our Heavenly goal. Jesus is the Son of God, the Light of the World, and eternal, not passing away like the sun and moon, the stars, or even the universe. The elevation of the Sacred Host—the Blessed Sacrament is like an eternal sunrise. Jesus in His Transfiguration and Resurrection is close to us—"Emman-uel—God with us." We adore and receive the Real Presence of Jesus.

May the sun and the moon remind us of the Mother of Jesus who is our Mother too, the Queen of Heaven who stands with the moon at her feet and the stars as a crown surrounding her head. May we honor her as our mother and listen for her inviting us to listen to the voice of her Son and to do whatever He tells us. May Mary shower graces from Heaven upon us like radiant gems and shining stars.

Jesus calls us the "light of the world" (Mt 5:14). How are we light to others? Do we let our light shine by good deeds and example? When we radiate God's Goodness through good works, Jesus shines through us. As a lamp is not hidden under a bushel basket but instead placed on the lamp stand for all to see, may we utilize our talents and gifts to spread God's Love in our families, work places, and communities. Then God's Light and Love will dispel the darkness of crime, terror, and war. The universe will be anew right here in this small corner, this earth shining brighter and radiating God's Goodness, a shiny blue and green gem.

*****

Joshua 10:13
So the sun and the moon stopped and stood still until Israel defeated its enemies. The sun stood still and didn't go down for about a whole day.

*****

Psalm 8:3
I often think of the heavens
your hands have made,
and of the moon and stars
you put in place.

*****

Psalm 104:19
You created the moon
to tell us the seasons.
The sun knows when to set...

*****

Psalm 121:6
You won't be harmed
by the sun during the day
or by the moon at night.

*****

Psalm 136:9
He lets the moon and the stars
rule each night.
God's love never fails.

*****

Luke 21:25
Strange things will happen to the sun, moon, and stars. The
nations on earth will be afraid of the roaring sea and tides, and they
won't know what to do...

*****

1 Corinthians 15:41 (NIV)
The sun has one kind of splendor, the moon another and the stars
another; and star differs from star in splendor.

*****

Revelation 12:1 (NIV)
A great and wondrous sign appeared in heaven: a woman clothed
with the sun, with the moon under her feet and a crown of twelve
stars on her head.

*****

Revelation 21:23
And the city did not need the sun or the moon. The glory of God
was shining on it, and the Lamb was its light.

*****

…I sing the wisdom that ordained
the sun to rule the day;
The moon shines full at God's command,
and all the stars obey.
—Isaac Watts (1674–1748). *I Sing the Mighty* Power *of God* (*Praise
for Creation and Providence*) [1715].

*****

He [the sun] gives light as soon as he rises.
—Benjamin Franklin (1706–1790). *An Economical Project* [1784].

*****

…Must in death your daylight finish? My sun sets to rise again.
—Robert Browning. *At the "Mermaid"* [1876], st. 10.

*****

I was continuing to shrink. To become, what? The infinitesimal?
What was I? Still a human being, or was I the man of the
future?…So close, the infinitesimal and the infinite, but suddenly I
knew they were really the two ends of the same concept. The unbelievably small and the unbelievably vast eventually meet, like the
closing of a gigantic circle. I looked up, as if somehow I would
grasp the heavens. The universe, worlds beyond number, God's silver tapestry spread across the night. And in that moment I knew
the answer to the riddle of the infinite. I had thought in terms of
man's own limited dimension. I had presumed upon nature. That
existence begins and ends is man's conception, not nature's, and I
felt my body dwindling, melting, becoming nothing. My fears
melted away and in their place came acceptance. All this vast majesty of creation—it had to mean something. And then I meant
something, too. Yes, smaller than the smallest—I meant some-

thing, too. To God, there is no zero. I still exist. Even athletes need to sleep.
  —Friedrich Dürrenmatt (1921–1990). Jack Arnold. trans. by Gerhard P. Knapp (1995). *Romulus the Great*, act I (1956). With Permission.

*****

Night unto night makes known God's message
The sun sets beneath the western horizon.
The blue sky grows black as daylight fades.
Bright stars shine brilliantly upon the night sky.
Planets wander about, chasing one another.

The sun's rays have gone and the earth becomes cold.
The clear, star-dusted dome covers the horizons.
Blue, green, white, yellow, orange, and red lights
Adorn the Heavens as light travels for eons to the earth.

The ground is cold; winds sweep the earth.
The constellations play their historic roles of myths.
The universe is vast and galaxies keep watch
As time passes upon the earth.

Bats flutter about in the darkness, searching for food.
Bullfrogs call out to each other; insects fly about.
Fish jump out of the warm waters to catch their food.
Loons call out their weird songs of laughter.

Squirrels and chipmunks scurry about, then find rest.
Ducks sleep in their nest; insects and arachnids go to work.
The spruce appear to catch fire by the rising moon.
The moon, large and full, begins its ever-continuous journey.

Although the earth turns and travels, we seem to be still.
The characters of stories dance about in the dome.

Constellations rise and fall
Then disappear below the horizon.

Night hours pass quickly; time never sits still.
A faint glow appears along the eastern horizon.
Stars begin to disappear from sight.
The appearance of the rising sun ends the night.

A dense fog covers the waters and fleets over the shore.
Mist rises above the lake and travels about.
All God's creatures awaken and begin their day.
The sun will soon burn off the fog, as the earth warms again.
—Anthony R. Brach (1981).

*****

Simply looking up at the sky can uplift our minds and hearts. Beautiful sunrises and sunsets move us to awe and wonderment. Cloud formations and light phenomena, anticrepescular rays, light pillars, nacreous clouds, and eclipses fascinate us. Shooting stars—meteor showers, comets, and the moon in its waxing, full, and waning phases draw our attention. As we lift our eyes to the skies like the three wise men from the east, may we offer God our prayers of praise and thanks.

Despite its distance of 149.6 million kilometers, the sun lights and heats the earth. Sunlight produces ozone that protects life from harmful ultraviolet light. Solar storms, sunspots, and auroras remind us of the sun's enormous power, and our all-powerful Creator. May we seek ways to use solar energy efficiently and effectively to provide power, to light, heat, and cool our homes and communities.

4

The Rainbow and The Aurora

Noah's Ark.
Drawn by Rudolf Koch. Courtesy of Arion Press.

*****

The rainbow's colorful bands of red, orange, yellow, green, blue, indigo, and violet remind us of the promise of God's Providential care. Never will God destroy the earth by flood again as in the days of Noah. The rainbow serves as a reminder of our covenant, that God will always be there for us His people. Rainbows and auroras are magnificent signs of the joy and splendor of God. Rainbows stretching over the horizon are like bridges between peoples and nations, not barriers or walls. May we reconcile with God and one another. Rainbows are like God's smiles upon the earth and auroras like angels dancing in the night sky.

When things are difficult, when there is suffering in life, may we remember to look for rainbows and all signs and miracles of God's

Love around us. Our Loving God provides many "signal graces" along life's journey. If only we look with eyes of faith through the prism of life, we will see many wonders. May there be more "miracles of the sun" as at Fatima to inspire the hearts and minds of humankind.

*****

Genesis 9:12
The rainbow that I have put in the sky will be my sign to you and to every living creature on earth. It will remind you that I will keep this promise forever.

*****

Ezekiel 1:28
...as colorful as a rainbow that appears after a storm. I realized I was seeing the brightness of the LORD's glory! So I bowed with my face to the ground, and just then I heard a voice speaking to me.

*****

Revelation 4:3
The one who was sitting there sparkled like precious stones of jasper and carnelian. A rainbow that looked like an emerald surrounded the throne.

*****

Revelation 10:1
I saw another powerful angel come down from heaven. This one was covered with a cloud, and a rainbow was over his head. His face was like the sun, his legs were like columns of fire...

*****

My heart leaps up when I behold
A rainbow in the sky...
—William Wordsworth (1770–1850). *My Heart Leaps Up* [1807].

*****

When the lamp is shattered
The light in the dust lies dead—
When the cloud is scattered
The rainbow's glory is shed.
—Percy Bysshe Shelley (1792–1822). *When the Lamp is Shattered*
[1822], st. 1.

*****

It was a comfort in those succeeding days to sit up and contemplate the majestic panorama of mountains and valleys spread out below us and eat ham and hard boiled eggs while our spiritual natures reveled alternately in rainbows, thunderstorms, and peerless sunsets…
—Mark Twain [Samuel Langhorne Clemens] (1835–1910). *Roughing It* [1871], p 139, American Publishing Company.

*****

The Immaculata is the Mediatrix of Graces. She is overflowing with grace, and we receive from that superabundance of grace.
—St. Maximilian Kolbe. *Aim Higher!: Spiritual and Marian reflections of St. Maximilian Kolbe.* Prow Books / Franciscan Marytown Press.

*****

O divine Spirit…renew in our own days your miracles as of a second Pentecost.
—Pope John XXIII (1881–1963). (VIS—Vatican Information Service). With permission.

*****

May we be alert for every divine grace that arrives sometimes as unexpectedly and as surprising as rainbows and auroras. May we cooperate with God's Will—His Plan for us at the moment, whether it be preparing a meal, washing dishes, cleaning the house, weeding a garden, or reviewing spelling words with a child. Then watch for God's smile reflected in the smiles of our loved ones and in the flowers of the garden. May that joy renew us and shine through us to our families, friends, co-workers, community, nation, and the entire world. As those rainbows and auroras touch every heart upon the earth, all will be aware of His Love.

5

Seasons

With the tilt of the earth on its axis, its orbit, and the changing angle of the sun, we are blessed with the seasons, and day and night. Spring flowers and the morning sunrise remind us of new life at Easter. We spend the longer sunny days in the heat of summer trying to stay cool while working or recreating, visiting parks, gardens, mountains, and shores. Falling autumn leaves warn of the approach of winter, and the dusk of nightfall signals the passing of time. The shorter cold days of winter and the darkness of night remind us of the shortness of life and the end times; however, during the darkest days, the celebration of Christmas reminds us of the birth of the Christ Child—the Light of the world. Though the seasons are ever changing and time passes from night to day, God's Love is constant and eternal. May we be steadfast and faithful in our love of God, family, and neighbor.

*****

Exodus 34:21
Do your work in six days and rest on the seventh day, even during the seasons for plowing and harvesting.

*****

Leviticus 26:4
...and I will send rain to make your crops grow and your trees produce fruit.

*****

Deuteronomy 11:14–15
…he will send rain at the right seasons, so you will have more than enough food, wine, and olive oil, and there will be plenty of grass for your cattle.

*****

Deuteronomy 28:12
The LORD will open the storehouses of the skies where he keeps the rain, and he will send rain on your land at just the right times. He will make you successful in everything you do. You will have plenty of money to lend to other nations, but you won't need to borrow any yourself.

*****

Job 5:26 (NIV)
You will come to the grave in full vigor, like sheaves gathered in season.

*****

Job 6:17
…then suddenly disappear in the summer heat.

*****

Job 38:32 (NIV)
Can you bring forth the constellations in their seasons or lead out the Bear with its cubs?

*****

Psalm 1:3
They are like trees
growing beside a stream,
trees that produce
fruit in season
and always have leaves.

Those people succeed
in everything they do.

*****

Psalm 90: 1, 4–6, 12
Our Lord, in all generations you have been our home....but a
thousand years mean nothing to you! They are merely a day gone
by or a few hours in the night. You bring our lives to an end just
like a dream. We are merely tender grass that sprouts and grows in
the morning, but dries up by evening....Teach us to use wisely all
the time we have.

*****

Psalm 104:19
You created the moon
to tell us the seasons.
The sun knows when to set...

*****

Ecclesiastes 3:1
Everything on earth has its own time and its own season.

*****

Song of Solomon 2:12
...flowers cover the earth,
it's time to sing.
The cooing of doves
is heard in our land.

*****

Jeremiah 8:7
Storks, doves, swallows, and thrushes all know when it's time to fly
away for the winter and when to come back. But you, my people,
don't know what I demand.

*****

Ezekiel 34:26 (NIV)
I will bless them and the places surrounding my hill. I will send down showers in season; there will be showers of blessing.

*****

Daniel 2:21 (NIV)
He changes times and seasons; he sets up kings and deposes them. He gives wisdom to the wise and knowledge to the discerning.

*****

Mark 11:13
From a distance Jesus saw a fig tree covered with leaves, and he went to see if there were any figs on the tree. But there were not any, because it wasn't the season for figs.

*****

Acts 14:17 (NIV)
Yet he has not left himself without testimony: He has shown kindness by giving you rain from heaven and crops in their seasons; he provides you with plenty of food and fills your hearts with joy.

*****

Galatians 4:10
You even celebrate certain days, months, seasons, and years.

*****

2 Timothy 4:2 (NIV)
Preach the Word; be prepared in season and out of season; correct, rebuke and encourage—with great patience and careful instruction.

*****

Titus 1:3 (NIV)
…and at his appointed season he brought his word to light through the preaching entrusted to me by the command of God our Savior…

*****

In those vernal seasons of the year, when the air is calm and pleasant, it were an injury and sullenness against Nature not to go out, and see her riches, and partake in her rejoicing with heaven and earth.
—John Milton. *Tractate of Education* [1644].

*****

If we had no winter, the spring would not be so pleasant; if we did not sometimes taste of adversity, prosperity would not be so welcome.
—Anne Bradstreet (c. 1612–1672). *Meditations Divine and Moral* [1664], 3.

*****

A thousand ages in Thy sight
Are like an evening gone;
Short as the watch that ends the night
Before the rising sun.
—Isaac Watts. *O God, Our Help in Ages Past* (*The Psalms of David*) [1719].

*****

Therefore all seasons shall be sweet to thee,
Whether the summer clothe the general earth
With greenness, or the redbreast sit and sing
Betwixt the tufts of snow on the bare branch
Of mossy apple-tree, while the nigh thatch
Smokes in the sun-thaw; whether the eave-drops fall
Heard only in the trances of the blast,
Or if the secret ministry of frost
Shall hang them up in silent icicles,
Quietly shining to the quiet moon.
—Samuel Taylor Coleridge (1772–1834). *Frost at Midnight* [1798], 65.

*****

O, Wind, If Winter comes, can Spring be far behind?
—Percy Bysshe Shelley. *Ode to the West Wind* [1819], l. 69–70.

*****

While I enjoy the friendship of the seasons I trust that nothing can make life a burden to me.
—Henry David Thoreau (1817–1862). *Walden* [1854], in *The Writings of Henry David Thoreau*, vol. 2, p. 145, Houghton Mifflin (1906).

*****

Dear children, we now have lovely Spring days; the sun with its warming rays awakens everything to life, and the grass grows beautifully from the earth, the flowers take on colors, and, in a word, all this enraptures a human being. So, too, dear children, in our life and in our soul, Springtime should arise. The sun, which is God, should send its warmth flowing forth into our soul with its rays. Those rays are Mary; the warmth flowing forth from the sun should warm our hearts, so that in our soul much good would grow, and the flowers of virtue unfold and blossom....let us beg the Immaculata that she herself would plant the flowers of virtue in our hearts and that these flowers would bloom to God's greater glory.
—St. Maximilian Kolbe. *Will to Love—Reflections for Daily Living by St. Maximilian Kolbe, "Prophet of the Civilization of Love."* Marytown Press. With permission.

*****

Spring
As the morning's sunlight
grows brighter
As the crows awaken and caw
As the songbirds begin a symphony
The floral display is revealed.
Crocus petals unfold

Tulips stand proud and tall,
The morning dew disappears
The fog fades above.
Squirrels scurry about
Searching for seeds and nuts
The fauna feast on new blades of grass and sedges
On seeds, nuts, and fermented berries.
Geese rise together and
Flock northward
Continuing a long journey
Robins, blue jays, cardinals
Proclaim their territories.
Nests are built and remade
By many species of birds
Showers water the fields
For the planting by farmers
Nature proceeds without
Notions of what people are doing.
We are small, compared to the
Chief Spring Creator.
—Anthony R. Brach (1981).

Dicentra eximia (Ker Gawl.) Torr.—wild bleeding heart.
Photo courtesy of Paul G. Brach.

6

Earth

The Divine Meal.
Drawn by Rudolf Koch. Courtesy of Arion Press.

*****

As a child is fascinated with a globe, may we treasure the earth. About 4.6 billion years ago, God created this planet Earth to be our home, the marvelous "blue marble", an ark for us journeying through time and space to our eternal home. We live in this unique, habitable world with just the right atmosphere and temperature for life. Within the global ecosystem, the biosphere, we are blessed with water and soil, abundant resources, diverse plants and animals, and humankind.

God designed the earth as our home. Do we take care of our home? What are we doing to protect, conserve, and restore our air, water, and soil resources?

Two thousand years ago, Jesus of Nazareth, the Son of God, fully God and fully man, lived and walked upon this same earth, breathed the same air, drank the same water, and taught us about His Father. In the Holy Sacrifice of the Mass, ordinary gifts grown upon and harvested from the earth are changed into the Real Presence—Body, Blood, Soul, and Divinity of Jesus. Like Moses when he spoke with God in the burning bush, and Peter, James, and John when Jesus was transfigured on Mount Tabor, we are "standing on holy ground" (Exodus 3:5).

*****

Genesis 8:22
As long as the earth remains, there will be planting and harvest, cold and heat; winter and summer, day and night.

*****

Ezekiel 43:2 (NIV)
…and I saw the glory of the God of Israel coming from the east. His voice was like the roar of rushing waters, and the land was radiant with his glory.

*****

Isaiah 44:23
Tell the heavens and the earth to start singing! Tell the mountains and every tree in the forest to join in the song! The LORD has rescued his people; now they will worship him.

*****

Isaiah 49:13
Tell the heavens and the earth to celebrate and sing; command

every mountain to join in the song. The LORD's people have suffered, but he has shown mercy and given them comfort.

*****

Isaiah 55:12
When you are set free, you will celebrate and travel home in peace. Mountains and hills will sing as you pass by, and trees will clap.

*****

Isaiah 65:17
I am creating new heavens and a new earth; everything of the past will be forgotten.

*****

Isaiah 66:1
The LORD said: Heaven is my throne; the earth is my footstool. What kind of house could you build for me? In what place will I rest?

*****

Habakkuk 2:14 (NIV)
For the earth will be filled with the knowledge of the glory of the Lord, as the waters cover the sea.

*****

Matthew 5:5
God blesses those people who are humble. The earth will belong to them!

*****

Matthew 5:13
You are like salt for everyone on earth. But if salt no longer tastes like salt, how can it make food salty? All it is good for is to be thrown out and walked on.

*****

Matthew 5:18
Heaven and earth may disappear. But I promise you that not even a period or comma will ever disappear from the Law. Everything written in it must happen.

*****

Matthew 5:35
The earth is God's footstool, so don't swear by the earth. Jerusalem is the city of the great king, so don't swear by it.

*****

Matthew 6:10 (NIV)
…your kingdom come, your will be done on earth as it is in heaven.

*****

Matthew 6:19
Don't store up treasures on earth! Moths and rust can destroy them, and thieves can break in and steal them.

*****

Matthew 9:6
"…But I will show you that the Son of Man has the right to forgive sins here on earth." So Jesus said to the man, "Get up! Pick up your mat and go on home."

*****

Matthew 12:40
He (Jonah) was in the stomach of a big fish for three days and nights, just as the Son of Man will be deep in the earth for three days and nights.

*****

Matthew 16:19
I will give you the keys to the kingdom of heaven, and God in heaven will allow whatever you allow on earth. But he will not allow anything that you don't allow.

*****

Matthew 18:19
I promise that when any two of you on earth agree about something you are praying for, my Father in heaven will do it for you.

*****

Matthew 23:9
Don't call anyone on earth your father. All of you have the same Father in heaven.

*****

Matthew 24:30
Then a sign will appear in the sky. And there will be the Son of Man. All nations on earth will weep when they see the Son of Man coming on the clouds of heaven with power and great glory.

*****

Matthew 24:35
The sky and the earth won't last forever, but my words will.

*****

Matthew 27:51
At once the curtain in the temple was torn in two from top to bottom. The earth shook, and rocks split apart.

*****

Matthew 28:18
Jesus came to them and said: I have been given all authority in heaven and on earth!

*****

Luke 2:14 (NIV)
Glory to God in the highest, and on earth peace to men on whom his favor rests.

*****

John 3:12
If you don't believe when I talk to you about things on earth, how can you possibly believe if I talk to you about things in heaven?

*****

John 3:31
God's Son comes from heaven and is above all others. Everyone who comes from the earth belongs to the earth and speaks about earthly things. The one who comes from heaven is above all others.

*****

John 12:32 (NIV)
But I, when I am lifted up from the earth, will draw all men to myself.

*****

John 17:4
I have brought glory to you here on earth by doing everything you gave me to do.

*****

Acts 1:8
"…But the Holy Spirit will come upon you and give you power. Then you will tell everyone about me in Jerusalem, in all Judea, in Samaria, and everywhere in the world."

*****

Acts 2:19
I will work miracles in the sky above and wonders on the earth below. There will be blood and fire and clouds of smoke.

*****

Acts 3:25
You are really the ones God told his prophets to speak to. And you were given the promise that God made to your ancestors. He said to Abraham, "All nations on earth will be blessed because of someone from your family."

*****

Acts 7:49
Heaven is my throne, and the earth is my footstool. What kind of house will you build for me? In what place will I rest?

*****

Acts 10:11
He saw heaven open, and something came down like a huge sheet held up by its four corners.

*****

Acts 13:47
The Lord has given us this command, "I have placed you here as a light for the Gentiles. You are to take the saving power of God to people everywhere on earth."

*****

Acts 17:24
This God made the world and everything in it. He is Lord of heaven and earth, and he doesn't live in temples built by human hands.

*****

1 Corinthians 4:13 (NIV)
when we are slandered, we answer kindly. Up to this moment we
have become the scum of the earth, the refuse of the world.

*****

1 Corinthians 10:26
The Scriptures say, "The earth and everything in it belong to the
Lord."

*****

1 Corinthians 15:40
Everything in the heavens has a body, and so does everything on
earth. But each one is very different from all the others.

*****

1 Corinthians 15:47–49
The first man was made from the dust of the earth, but the second
man came from heaven. Everyone on earth has a body like the
body of the one who was made from the dust of the earth. And
everyone in heaven has a body like the body of the one who came
from heaven. Just as we are like the one who was made out of earth,
we will be like the one who came from heaven.

*****

2 Corinthians 5:1
Our bodies are like tents that we live in here on earth. But when
these tents are destroyed, we know that God will give each of us a
place to live. These homes will not be buildings that someone has
made, but they are in heaven and will last forever.

*****

Ephesians 1:10
Then when the time is right, God will do all that he has planned,
and Christ will bring together everything in heaven and on earth.

*****

Ephesians 3:15
All beings in heaven and on earth receive their life from him.

*****

Ephesians 4:9
When it says, "he went up," it means that Christ had been deep in the earth.

*****

Ephesians 6:3 (NIV)
…and you will have a long and happy life.

*****

Philippians 2:10
So at the name of Jesus everyone will bow down, those in heaven, on earth, and under the earth.

*****

Philippians 3:19 (NIV)
Their destiny is destruction, their god is their stomach, and their glory is in their shame. Their mind is on earthly things.

*****

Colossians 1:16
Everything was created by him, everything in heaven and on earth, everything seen and unseen, including all forces and powers, and all rulers and authorities. All things were created by God's Son, and everything was made for him.

*****

Colossians 1:20
And God was pleased for him to make peace by sacrificing his blood on the cross, so that all beings in heaven and on earth would be brought back to God.

*****

Colossians 3:2
Think about what is up there, not about what is here on earth.

*****

Colossians 3:5 (NIV)
Put to death, therefore, whatever belongs to your earthly nature: sexual immorality, impurity, lust, evil desires and greed, which is idolatry.

*****

Hebrews 1:10
The Scriptures also say, "In the beginning, Lord, you were the one who laid the foundation of the earth and created the heavens…"

*****

Hebrews 5:7 (NIV)
During the days of Jesus' life on earth, he offered up prayers and petitions with loud cries and tears to the one who could save him from death, and he was heard because of his reverent submission.

*****

Hebrews 11:13
Every one of those people died. But they still had faith, even though they had not received what they had been promised. They were glad just to see these things from far away, and they agreed that they were only strangers and foreigners on this earth.

*****

Hebrews 12:26
When God spoke the first time, his voice shook only the earth. This time he has promised to shake the earth once again, and heaven too.

*****

James 5:5
While here on earth, you have thought only of filling your own stomachs and having a good time. But now you are like fat cattle on their way to be butchered.

*****

James 5:18 (NIV)
Again he prayed, and the heavens gave rain, and the earth produced its crops.

*****

2 Peter 3:5
They will say this because they want to forget that long ago the heavens and the earth were made at God's command. The earth came out of water and was made from water.

*****

2 Peter 3:10, 13 (NIV)
But the day of the Lord will come like a thief. The heavens will disappear with a roar; the elements will be destroyed by fire, and the earth and everything in it will be laid bare. But in keeping with his promise we are looking forward to a new heaven and a new earth, the home of righteousness.

*****

Revelation 1:7
Look! He is coming with the clouds. Everyone will see him, even the ones who stuck a sword through him. All people on earth will weep because of him. Yes, it will happen! Amen.

*****

Revelation 3:10
You obeyed my message and endured. So I will protect you from the time of testing that everyone in all the world must go through.

*****

Revelation 5:3

No one in heaven or on earth or under the earth was able to open the scroll or see inside it.

*****

Revelation 5:10

"…You let them become kings and serve God as priests, and they will rule on earth."

*****

Revelation 5:13

Then I heard all beings in heaven and on the earth and under the earth and in the sea offer praise. Together, all of them were saying, "Praise, honor, glory, and strength forever and ever to the one who sits on the throne and to the Lamb!"

*****

Joy to the world! the Lord is come;
Let earth receive her King.
Let every heart prepare Him room,
And heav'n and nature sing.
—Isaac Watts. *Psalm 98* [1719], st. 1.

*****

The earth is not a mere fragment of dead history, stratum upon stratum like the leaves of a book, to be studied by geologists and antiquaries chiefly, but living poetry like the leaves of a tree, which precede flowers and fruit,—not a fossil earth, but a living earth; compared with whose great central life all animal and vegetable life is merely parasitic.
—Henry David Thoreau. *Walden* [1854], in *The Writings of Henry David Thoreau*, vol. 2, pp. 340–341, Houghton Mifflin (1906).

*****

Earth is here so kind, that just tickle her with a hoe and she laughs with a harvest.

—Douglas Jerrold (1803–1857). *"A Land of Plenty,"* *The Wit and Opinions of Douglas Jerrold* [1859].

*****

God gives all men all earth to love,
But, since man's heart is small,
Ordains for each one spot shall prove
Belovèd over all...
—Rudyard Kipling (1865–1936). *Sussex* [1902].

*****

The power and drama of the earth's forces draw our curiosity and wonder. Earthquakes and erupting volcanoes are amazing displays of power yet sources of potential danger. May emergency systems be developed to better warn, protect, and rescue people from danger. At the same time, the interior heat of the earth presents a source of geothermal energy, an alternate source to the limited supply of fossil fuels stored within this same earth. May we care for the earth and use its resources wisely.

7

Mountains and Hills

There is something about a mountain or hill, which beckons us to marvel at its immensity and for many to climb it. While climbing, we are focused upon the summit as our goal. Upon reaching the top, we are proud of our achievement and thankful to be there. Looking out as far as we can see toward the horizons, we are humbled by the grandeur of it all. A mountain can be a perfect place to retreat from the busyness of the day, to rest and pray in silence and peace. Jesus often went to a mountain to pray. Then He went about doing good works, healing the sick, and forgiving sins. Similarly, may our consciousness of God's Presence in silent prayer and at Mass, while in the outdoors or on retreat, and during recreation re-energize us to take care of those entrusted to us and to do good works.

*****

Genesis 49:26
My son, the blessings I give are better than the promise of ancient mountains or eternal hills. Joseph, I pray these blessings will come to you, because you are the leader of your brothers.

*****

Deuteronomy 33:15
You will have a rich harvest from the slopes of the ancient hills.

*****

Psalm 36:6
Your decisions are always fair.
They are firm like mountains,
deep like the sea,
and all people and animals
are under your care.

*****

Psalm 46:2
And so, we won't be afraid!
Let the earth tremble
and the mountains tumble
into the deepest sea.

*****

Psalm 46:3
Let the ocean roar and foam,
and its raging waves
shake the mountains.

*****

Psalm 72:3 (NIV)
The mountains will bring prosperity to the people,
the hills the fruit of righteousness.

*****

Psalm 80:10
Shade from this vine covered
the mountains.
Its branches
climbed
the mighty cedars…

*****

Psalm 104:13
From your home above

you send rain on the hills
and water the earth.

*****

Psalm 114:4 (NIV)
…the mountains skipped like rams,
the hills like lambs.

*****

Proverbs 8:25
My birth was before mountains were formed or hills were put in place.

*****

Song of Solomon 2:8
She Speaks:
I hear the voice
of the one I love,
as he comes leaping
over mountains and hills…

*****

Isaiah 2:2
In the future, the mountain with the LORD's temple will be the highest of all. It will reach above the hills; every nation will rush to it.

*****

Isaiah 40:12
Did any of you measure the ocean by yourself or stretch out the sky with your own hands? Did you put the soil of the earth in a bucket or weigh the hills and mountains on balance scales?

*****

Isaiah 42:15
I will destroy the mountains and what grows on them; I will dry up rivers and ponds.

*****

Isaiah 52:7 (NIV)
How beautiful on the mountains are the feet of those who bring good news, who proclaim peace, who bring good tidings, who proclaim salvation, who say to Zion, "Your God reigns!"

*****

Isaiah 54:10
Every mountain and hill may disappear. But I will always be kind and merciful to you; I won't break my agreement to give your nation peace.

*****

Isaiah 55:12
When you are set free, you will celebrate and travel home in peace. Mountains and hills will sing as you pass by, and trees will clap.

*****

Joel 3:18
On that day, fruitful vineyards will cover the mountains. And your cattle and goats that graze on the hills will produce a lot of milk. Streams in Judah will never run dry; a stream from my house will flow in Acacia Valley.

*****

Amos 9:13
You will have such a harvest that you won't be able to bring in all of your wheat before plowing time. You will have grapes left over from season to season; your fruitful vineyards will cover the mountains.

*****

Micah 4:1

In the future, the mountain with the LORD's temple will be the highest of all. It will reach above the hills, and every nation will rush to it.

*****

Micah 6:1

The LORD said to his people: Come and present your case to the hills and mountains.

*****

Nahum 1:5

At the sight of the LORD, mountains and hills tremble and melt; the earth and its people shudder and shake.

*****

Habakkuk 3:6

When you stopped, the earth shook; when you stared, nations trembled; when you walked along your ancient paths, eternal mountains and hills crumbled and collapsed.

*****

Matthew 14:23

Then he went up on a mountain where he could be alone and pray. Later that evening, he was still there.

*****

I sing the mighty power of God,
that made the mountains rise...
—Isaac Watts. *I Sing the Mighty Power of God* (*Praise for Creation and Providence*) [1715].

*****

And did those feet in ancient time
Walk upon England's mountains green?...
—William Blake (1757–1827). *Milton* [c. 1809], *prefactory poem.*

*****

All the hills blush; I think that autumn must be the best season to journey over even the Green Mountains. You frequently exclaim to yourself, What red maples!
—Henry David Thoreau. *"A Yankee in Canada"* [1853], in *The Writings of Henry David Thoreau*, vol. 5, p. 6, Houghton Mifflin (1906).

*****

Mountains are earth's undecaying monuments.
—Nathaniel Hawthorne (1804–1864). *Sketches from Memory* [1868], *The Notch of the White Mountains.*

*****

When our daily tasks and duties become hills of paper, and when the mountains in life are difficult to climb, may we remember that Jesus prayed at the Mount of Olives, carried His Cross up to Calvary, and died there for the forgiveness of our sins. He rose from the dead and ascended to Heaven where He is seated—higher than every hill and mountain.

Glacier National Park, British Columbia.
Photo courtesy of Paul G. Brach.

8

The Rock

God is our Rock. He is our refuge and our firm foundation. As Moses drew water from the rock in the desert, Jesus gives us Living Water for eternity. Jesus, the stone rejected by the builders is the Cornerstone, the Rock of our salvation. Jesus called Simon son of John, "Cephas" (Jn 1:42) or Peter, to be the rock upon which He built His Church. May God bless our Holy Father the Pope and all the Church. May the Church continue to do the work of Christ upon the earth. May God bless our homes and cities that we may dwell upon His sure foundation.

The Kingdom of God is the "pearl of great price" (Mt 13:45). Hidden within the oyster shell, the pearl awaits its discovery and purchase. How can we purchase this perfect, priceless pearl today? God loves those of a humble spirit. May we offer our daily sacrifice of prayer, fasting, and good works. We can become better aware of God's Presence and pray at all times, morning, noon, evening, and night. We can fast from sin and selfishness, from complaining and being overly critical. We can fast from dark deeds and put on the armor of light Christ Himself. We can serve others at home, work, and in our towns and cities.

Jesus calls us the "salt of the earth" (Mt 5:13). In our conversations and activities, do we add just the right kind and amount of seasoning? Do we think before writing? Do we listen before speaking? Do we wait before criticizing? Do we offer generous amounts of praise and thanksgiving? Or do we wait until it is too late to do so? May we provide the right salt to season our relationships in our families, work, and communities.

May we be the "living stones" (1 Pt 2:5) that build up and support the Church. May we be steadfast in our commitment like Jesus, the Rock. We share the "sign of peace." Human chains are made up of clasped hands and linked arms. Likewise, together may all of us living stones fitted together form a beautiful structure, the Church, the Kingdom of God here on earth, a kingdom of love, justice and peace.

*****

Exodus 17:6 (NIV)
"…I will stand there before you by the rock at Horeb. Strike the rock, and water will come out of it for the people to drink." So Moses did this in the sight of the elders of Israel.

*****

Exodus 33:21–22
There is a rock not far from me. Stand beside it, and before I pass by in all of my shining glory, I will put you in a large crack in the rock. I will cover your eyes with my hand until I have passed by.

*****

Deuteronomy 8:8–9, 15
You can dig for copper in those hills, and the stones are made of iron ore. And you won't go hungry. Wheat and barley fields are everywhere, and so are vineyards and orchards full of fig, pomegranate, and olive trees, and there is plenty of honey. Remember how he led you in that huge and frightening desert where poisonous snakes and scorpions live. There was no water, but the LORD split open a rock, and water poured out so you could drink.

*****

Deuteronomy 32:4, 13
The LORD is a mighty rock, and he never does wrong. God can always be trusted to bring justice. Your fields were rich with grain.

Olive trees grew in your stony soil, and honey was found among the rocks.

*****

2 Samuel 22:2–3
Our LORD and our God, you are my mighty rock, my fortress, my protector. You are the rock where I am safe. You are my shield, my powerful weapon, and my place of shelter. You rescue me and keep me from being hurt.

*****

2 Samuel 22:32, 47
You alone are God! Only you are a mighty rock. You are the living LORD! I will praise you! You are a mighty rock. I will honor you for keeping me safe.

*****

1 Kings 19:11
"Go out and stand on the mountain," the LORD replied. "I want you to see me when I pass by." All at once, a strong wind shook the mountain and shattered the rocks. But the LORD was not in the wind. Next, there was an earthquake, but the LORD was not in the earthquake.

*****

Nehemiah 9:15
When they were hungry, you sent bread from heaven, and when they were thirsty, you let water flow from a rock. Then you commanded them to capture the land that you had solemnly promised.

*****

Job 39:28 (NIV)
He dwells on a cliff and stays there at night; a rocky crag is his stronghold.

*****

Psalm 18:2, 31, 46
You are my mighty rock,
my fortress, my protector,
the rock where I am safe,
my shield,
my powerful weapon,
and my place of shelter.
You alone are God!
Only you are a mighty rock.
You are the living LORD!
I will praise you.
You are a mighty rock.
I will honor you
for keeping me safe.

*****

Psalm 19:14
Let my words and my thoughts
be pleasing to you, LORD,
because you are my mighty rock
and my protector.

*****

Psalm 27:5
In times of trouble,
you will protect me.
You will hide me in your tent
and keep me safe
on top of a mighty rock.

*****

Psalm 28:1
Only you, LORD,
are a mighty rock!
Don't refuse to help me
when I pray.

If you don't answer me,
I will soon be dead.

*****

Psalm 31:2–3
Listen to my prayer
and hurry to save me.
Be my mighty rock
and the fortress
where I am safe.
You, LORD God,
are my mighty rock
and my fortress.
Lead me and guide me,
so that your name
will be honored.

*****

Psalm 40:2
...and pulled me
from a lonely pit
full of mud and mire.
You let me stand on a rock
with my feet firm...

*****

Psalm 42:9
You are my mighty rock.
Why have you forgotten me?
Why must enemies mistreat me
and make me sad?

*****

Psalm 61:2
I feel hopeless,
and I cry out to you

from a faraway land.
Lead me to the mighty rock
high above me.

*****

Psalm 62:2, 7
God alone is the mighty rock
that keeps me safe
and the fortress
where I am secure.
God saves me and honors me.
He is that mighty rock
where I find safety.

*****

Psalm 78:15–16
God made water flow
from rocks
he split open
in the desert,
and his people drank freely,
as though from a lake.
He made streams gush out
like rivers from rocks.

*****

Psalm 78:35
They remembered God Most High,
the mighty rock
that kept them safe.

*****

Psalm 81:16 (NIV)
"…But you would be fed
with the finest of wheat;

with honey from the rock
I would satisfy you."

*****

Psalm 94:22
You, LORD God, are my fortress,
that mighty rock
where I am safe.

*****

Psalm 95:1
Sing joyful songs to the LORD!
Praise the mighty rock
where we are safe.

*****

Psalm 105:41
God even split open a rock,
and streams of water
gushed into the desert.

*****

Psalm 114:8
…because he turns solid rock
into flowing streams
and pools of water.

*****

Song of Solomon 2:14
You are my dove
hiding among the rocks
on the side of a cliff.
Let me see how lovely you are!
Let me hear the sound
of your melodious voice.

*****

Isaiah 2:10, 19
Every one of you, go hide among the rocks and in the ground, because the LORD is fearsome, marvelous, and glorious. You had better hide in caves and holes—the LORD will be fearsome, marvelous, and glorious when he comes to terrify people on earth.

*****

Isaiah 8:14 (NIV)
…and he will be a sanctuary; but for both houses of Israel he will be a stone that causes men to stumble and a rock that makes them fall. And for the people of Jerusalem he will be a trap and a snare.

*****

Isaiah 26:4
So always trust the LORD because he is forever our mighty rock.

*****

Isaiah 32:2
They will be a place of safety from stormy winds, a stream in the desert, and a rock that gives shade from the heat of the sun.

*****

Isaiah 44:8
Don't tremble with fear! Didn't I tell you long ago? Didn't you hear me? I alone am God—no one else is a mighty rock.

*****

Isaiah 48:21
He led us through the desert and made water flow from a rock to satisfy our thirst.

*****

Isaiah 51:1
If you want to do right and obey the LORD, follow Abraham's example. He was the rock from which you were chipped.

*****

Jeremiah 23:29
My words are a powerful fire; they are a hammer that shatters rocks.

*****

Daniel 2:34–35
As you watched, a stone was cut from a mountain—but not by human hands. The stone struck the feet, completely shattering the iron and clay. Then the iron, the clay, the bronze, the silver, and the gold were crushed and blown away without a trace, like husks of wheat at threshing time. But the stone became a tremendous mountain that covered the entire earth.

*****

Zechariah 12:3
But I will turn Jerusalem into a heavy stone that crushes anyone who tries to lift it. When all nations on earth surround Jerusalem...

*****

Matthew 7:24–25
Anyone who hears and obeys these teachings of mine is like a wise person who built a house on solid rock. Rain poured down, rivers flooded, and winds beat against that house. But it did not fall, because it was built on solid rock.

*****

Matthew 16:18
So I will call you Peter, which means "a rock." On this rock I will build my church, and death itself will not have any power over it.

*****

Matthew 27:51

At once the curtain in the temple was torn in two from top to bottom. The earth shook, and rocks split apart.

*****

Matthew 27:60

Then Joseph put the body in his own tomb that had been cut into solid rock and had never been used. He rolled a big stone against the entrance to the tomb and went away.

*****

Luke 8:6

Other seeds fell on rocky ground and started growing. But the plants did not have enough water and soon dried up.

*****

Luke 8:13

The seeds that fell on rocky ground are the people who gladly hear the message and accept it. But they don't have deep roots, and they believe only for a little while. As soon as life gets hard, they give up.

*****

Romans 9:33

…just as God says in the Scriptures, "Look! I am placing in Zion a stone to make people stumble and fall. But those who have faith in that one will never be disappointed."

*****

1 Corinthians 10:4

…and drank the same spiritual drink, which flowed from the spiritual rock that followed them. That rock was Christ.

*****

1 Peter 2:8
They disobeyed the message and stumbled and fell over that stone, because they were doomed.

*****

Revelation 6:15–16
The kings of the earth, its famous people, and its military leaders hid in caves or behind rocks on the mountains. They hid there together with the rich and the powerful and with all the slaves and free people. Then they shouted to the mountains and the rocks, "Fall on us! Hide us from the one who sits on the throne and from the anger of the Lamb…"

*****

Rock of Ages, cleft for me,
Let me hide myself in thee.
—Augustus Montague Toplady (1740–1778). *Rock of Ages* [1775], st. 1.

*****

The lichen on the rocks is a rude and simple shield which beginning and imperfect Nature suspended there. Still hangs her wrinkled trophy.
—Henry David Thoreau. *A Week on the Concord and Merrimack Rivers* [1849], in *The Writings of Henry David Thoreau*, vol. 1, p. 265, Houghton Mifflin (1906).

*****

When I am finishing a picture I hold some God-made object up to it—a rock, a flower, the branch of a tree or my hand—as a kind of final test. If the painting stands up beside a thing man cannot make, the painting is authentic. If there's a clash between the two, it is bad art.
—Marc Chagall (1889–1985). *Saturday Evening Post* (New York, 2 December 1962). Permission granted: Used with permission of The *Saturday Evening Post* Society c 1962 (Renewed).

*****

When we are humbled in spirit and recognize ourselves as servants of God and one another, we are like the rocks of this earth, which despite their hardness are subject to change. The forces of the earth, pressure and heat, wind and water erosion affect rocks. The parent material from broken, crushed, and eroded rocks is the foundation for mineral soils, sand, silt, clay, and sea salts. May we allow God—the Eternal Rock to change us and mold us into His instruments of peace, love, and hope. He can melt our "hearts of stone."

Chimney Bluffs on Lake Ontario, New York.

9

Wind

Wind—we do not know where it comes from or where it goes. We cannot see the wind yet we see its effects in the trees. We feel the coolness of the wind touching our faces, a refreshing, gentle breeze, reminding us of the breath of life. How wonderful it is to breathe, yet we do so unconsciously and involuntarily, from birth to death. Yet to focus upon our breathing, to be calm and aware of our surroundings and ourselves, we are ready to pray by calling to mind God's Presence. *Veni Sancti Spiritus*—Come Holy Spirit! May we be moved by the Holy Spirit to do God's Will. May we never be too busy for the Lord.

*****

Genesis 8:1
God did not forget about Noah and the animals with him in the boat. So God made a wind blow, and the water started going down.

*****

Exodus 14:21
Moses stretched his arm over the sea, and the LORD sent a strong east wind that blew all night until there was dry land where the water had been. The sea opened up...

*****

Numbers 11:31
Some time later the LORD sent a strong wind that blew quails in from the sea until Israel's camp was completely surrounded with birds, piled up about three feet high for miles in every direction.

*****

2 Samuel 22:11
You rode on the backs of flying creatures. You appeared with the wind as wings.

*****

1 Kings 19:11
"Go out and stand on the mountain," the LORD replied. "I want you to see me when I pass by." All at once, a strong wind shook the mountain and shattered the rocks. But the LORD was not in the wind. Next, there was an earthquake, but the LORD was not in the earthquake.

*****

Job 26:13 (NIV)
By his breath the skies became fair; his hand pierced the gliding serpent.

*****

Job 37:9 (NIV)
The tempest comes out from its chamber, the cold from the driving winds.

*****

Psalm 107:25
At his command a storm arose,
and waves covered the sea.

*****

Psalm 135:7
The LORD makes the clouds rise
from far across the earth,
and he makes lightning
to go with the rain.
Then from his secret place
he sends out the wind.

*****

Psalm 147:18
At his command the ice melts,
the wind blows,
and streams begin to flow.

*****

Isaiah 49:10
They won't go hungry or get thirsty; they won't be bothered by the scorching sun or hot desert winds. I will be merciful while leading them along to streams of water.

*****

Amos 4:13
I created the mountains and the wind. I let humans know what I am thinking. I bring darkness at dawn and step over hills. I am the LORD God All-Powerful!

*****

Matthew 8:26–27
But Jesus replied, "Why are you so afraid? You surely don't have much faith." Then he got up and ordered the wind and the waves to calm down. And everything was calm. The men in the boat were amazed and said, "Who is this? Even the wind and the waves obey him."

*****

Matthew 11:7 (NIV)
As John's disciples were leaving, Jesus began to speak to the crowd about John: "What did you go out into the desert to see? A reed swayed by the wind?…"

*****

Matthew 14:24, 30, 32
By this time the boat was a long way from the shore. It was going against the wind and was being tossed around by the waves.…But when Peter saw how strong the wind was, he was afraid and started sinking. "Save me, Lord!" he shouted. Right away, Jesus reached out his hand. He helped Peter up and said, "You surely don't have much faith. Why do you doubt?"…When Jesus and Peter got into the boat, the wind died down.

*****

John 3:8
Only God's Spirit gives new life. The Spirit is like the wind that blows wherever it wants to. You can hear the wind, but you don't know where it comes from or where it is going.

*****

Acts 2:2
Suddenly there was a noise from heaven like the sound of a mighty wind! It filled the house where they were meeting.

*****

If the east wind doesn't prevail over the west wind, then the west wind will prevail over east wind.
—Chinese proverb.

*****

A wind came up out of the sea, And said, "O mists, make room for me."
—Henry Wadsworth Longfellow (1809–1882). *Daybreak* (l. 1–2).

"My eyes are blinking," Dathi said,
"With the secrets of God half blind,
But I can see where the wind goes
And follow the way of the wind;
And blessedness goes where the wind goes…."
—William Butler Yeats (1865–1939). "*The Blessed*" [1899].

*****

Powerful winds can be awesome but also disastrous. Tornadoes, gales, and hurricanes have uprooted the homes and lives of many. Improved education, emergency preparedness, and early warnings are essential for survival. May we be generous in offering support and help to victims of disasters. At the same time, the power of the wind presents a renewable source of energy. Windmills and wind-driven generators have proven useful for harnessing this energy. May we like the windmills rotate and spin with the Love of God, so that we may "go forth to love and serve the Lord by loving and serving one another."

Photo Credit: US National Oceanic and Atmospheric Administration.

10

Water

Water covers about 70% of the earth's surface and amounts to a total water supply of about 326 million cubic miles. Water refreshes and gives life, renews and washes clean. The Lord is our Shepherd who leads us to restful and refreshing waters. Through Baptism, we have died to self and risen from the waters to new life in Christ. When newly blessed Holy Water is sprinkled upon us at Easter, we recall our Baptism. As Holy Water fonts from above, dew and rain can remind us of Jesus who is the Living Water who forever quenches our thirst when we seek Him. May we allow God to continually renew us through the Sacraments of Reconciliation and the Eucharist.

We must be born again from above. O God, You wash us with the purifying waters of Baptism. Jesus is the Living Water. Through the action of the Holy Spirit, we are reborn. We are a new creation, the children of God. As children at Christmas, we marvel at the birth of Jesus and hear the angels sing Hosanna to God in the Highest. Emmanuel—God is with us, now and always. "Hail Mary, full of grace, the Lord is with you. Blessed are you among women and blessed is the fruit of your womb, Jesus…" (Lk 1:28, 42).

*****

Genesis 27:28
God will bless you, my son, with dew from heaven and with fertile fields, rich with grain and grapes.

*****

Exodus 16:13–14
That evening a lot of quails came and landed everywhere in the camp, and the next morning dew covered the ground. After the dew had gone, the desert was covered with thin flakes that looked like frost.

*****

Deuteronomy 11:11
But the hills and valleys in the promised land are watered by rain from heaven…

*****

Deuteronomy 32:2
Israel, I will teach you. My words will be like gentle rain on tender young plants, or like dew on the grass.

*****

Deuteronomy 33:28
Israel, you will live in safety; your enemies will be gone. The dew will fall from the sky, and you will have plenty of grain and wine.

*****

Isaiah 55:10 (NIV)
As the rain and the snow come down from heaven, and do not return to it without watering the earth and making it bud and flourish, so that it yields seed for the sower and bread for the eater…

*****

Hosea 14:5
I will be like the dew—then you will blossom like lilies and have roots like a tree.

*****

Proverbs 8:24
When I was born, there were no oceans or springs of water.

*****

Job 37:6 (NIV)
He says to the snow, 'Fall on the earth,' and to the rain shower, 'Be a mighty downpour.'

*****

Job 38:28
Who is the father of the dew and of the rain?

*****

Psalm 23: 1–3
You, LORD, are my shepherd.
I will never be in need.
You let me rest in fields
of green grass.
You lead me to streams
of peaceful water,
and you refresh my life.
You are true to your name,
and you lead me
along the right paths.

*****

Psalm 104:10
You provide streams of water
in the hills and valleys…

*****

Matthew 4:18
While Jesus was walking along the shore of Lake Galilee, he saw two brothers. One was Simon, also known as Peter, and the other was Andrew. They were fishermen, and they were casting their net into the lake.

*****

Matthew 13:47
The kingdom of heaven is like what happens when a net is thrown into a lake and catches all kinds of fish.

*****

Matthew 14:25–26 (NIV)
During the fourth watch of the night Jesus went out to them, walking on the lake. When the disciples saw him walking on the lake, they were terrified. "It's a ghost," they said, and cried out in fear.

*****

Mark 2:13
Once again, Jesus went to the shore of Lake Galilee. A large crowd gathered around him,
and he taught them.

*****

Mark 4:1
The next time Jesus taught beside Lake Galilee, a big crowd gathered. It was so large that he had to sit in a boat out on the lake, while the people stood on the shore.

*****

John 4:10–11, 13–14
Jesus answered, "You don't know what God wants to give you, and you don't know who is asking you for a drink. If you did, you would ask me for the water that gives life." "Sir," the woman said, "you don't even have a bucket, and the well is deep. Where are you going to get this life-giving water?" Jesus answered, "Everyone who drinks this water will get thirsty again. But no one who drinks the water I give will ever be thirsty again. The water I give is like a flowing fountain that gives eternal life."

*****

John 6:16–17
That evening, Jesus' disciples went down to the lake. They got into a boat and started across for Capernaum. Later that evening Jesus had still not come to them…

*****

John 6:22–25
The people who had stayed on the east side of the lake knew that only one boat had been there. They also knew that Jesus had not left in it with his disciples. But the next day some boats from Tiberias sailed near the place where the crowd had eaten the bread for which the Lord had given thanks. They saw that Jesus and his disciples had left. Then they got into the boats and went to Capernaum to look for Jesus. They found him on the west side of the lake and asked, "Rabbi, when did you get here?"

*****

John 7:38
"…Have faith in me, and you will have life-giving water flowing from deep inside you, just as the Scriptures say."

*****

Revelation 7:17
The Lamb in the center of the throne will be their shepherd. He will lead them to streams of life-giving water, and God will wipe all tears from their eyes.

*****

When drinking water, think of its source.
—Chinese proverb.

*****

Little drops of water
Little grains of sand,
Make the mighty ocean
And the pleasant land.

—Julia A. Fletcher Carney (1823–1908). *Little Things* [1845], st. 1.

*****

The lack of water might well be the principal question that humanity will have to address in the near future. It is not enough to think of present needs; we have a serious responsibility to future generations, who will ask us to account for our commitment to safeguard the natural resources that the Creator has entrusted to us so that we treat them with care and respect.
—Pope John Paul II, 5 July 2000 (VIS—Vatican Information Service). With permission.

*****

God provides us with the rain. Water refreshes us, and is essential for drinking, cooking, and washing. We need to conserve this precious resource and prevent waste. Millions without sufficient clean water call out in thirst for safe drinking water. With all the advances of our technology, we can at least provide the means for them to reach life-sustaining water.

Powerful moving waters provide a source of renewable energy. Thousands of years ago, waterwheels were first used to convert potential energy to kinetic energy. Waves, tides, and waterfalls can power hydroelectric plants to provide energy to light our homes. However, dams built for the purpose have a record of problems. Natural sources of water power seem best.

Waves, surf, and storms can be awesome but also dangerous. Tidal waves have suddenly destroyed homes and lives. Rip tides have taken the lives of swimmers. Storms have flooded homes and communities. Early warning systems and education are necessary to protect lives. May we be charitable to victims of floods and disasters.

Blackwater Falls State Park, West Virginia.
Photo courtesy of Paul G. Brach.

11

Ice and Snow

The bright reflection of sunshine on ice and snow can remind us of the Light of the World. Ice and snow brighten the dark, gloomy days of winter. Icicles, frozen waterfalls, frost on windows, and intricate snowflakes are sculptures of beauty. We laugh with the children who build snowmen and snow angels, and sled and ski upon snowy hills. God is ever more refreshing than cold ocean waters or iced lemonade on a hot summer day. As snow blankets and insulates the earth in winter, may we be aware of God embracing us.

*****

Isaiah 1:18
I, the LORD, invite you to come and talk it over. Your sins are scarlet red, but they will be whiter than snow or wool.

*****

Psalm 51:7
Wash me with hyssop
until I am clean
and whiter than snow.

*****

Ezekiel 1:4
I saw a windstorm blowing in from the north. Lightning flashed

from a huge cloud and lit up the whole sky with a dazzling bright-ness. The fiery center of the cloud was as shiny as polished metal…

*****

Ezekiel 1: 22–23
Above the living creatures, I saw something that was sparkling like ice, and it reminded me of a dome. Each creature had two of its wings stretched out toward the creatures on either side, with the other two wings folded against its body.

*****

Psalm 147:16
He covers the ground with snow
like a blanket of wool,
and he scatters frost
like ashes on the ground.

*****

Daniel 7:9
Thrones were set up while I was watching, and the Eternal God took his place. His clothing and his hair were white as snow. His throne was a blazing fire with fiery wheels…

*****

Matthew 28:3
The angel looked as bright as lightning, and his clothes were white as snow.

*****

Revelation 1:14
His head and his hair were white as wool or snow, and his eyes looked like flames of fire.

*****

I see my way as birds their trackless way.
I shall arrive,—what time, what circuit first,
I ask not; but unless God send his hail
Or blinding fire-balls, sleet or stifling snow,
In some time, his good time, I shall arrive:
He guides me and the bird. In his good time.
—Robert Browning. *Paracelsus*. Part i.

*****

Snow was general all over Ireland. It was falling on every part of the dark central plain, on the treeless hills, falling softly upon the Bog of Allen and farther westward, softly falling into the dark mutinous Shannon waves. It was falling, too, upon every part of the lonely churchyard on the hill where Michael Furey lay buried. It lay thickly drifted on the crooked crosses and headstones, on the spears of the little gate, on the barren thorns. His soul swooned slowly as he heard the snow falling faintly through the universe, and faintly falling, like the descent of their last end, upon all the living and the dead.
—James Joyce (1882–1941). *Dubliners* [1916], *The Dead*.

*****

A stiff breeze helped blow the big bear swiftly along as the ice reverberated to the percussion drums (thundering booms) that is typical of frozen bodies of water in the deep freeze of mid-winter. It was a delightful time. He wished that his friends back in western New York could hear the classical drum sounds, but he knew that this kind of magic was reserved for the "crazy" folk who love the deep woods in winter.
—Paul J. Brach (1999). With Permission.

Snowman and children.

12

Lightning and Fire

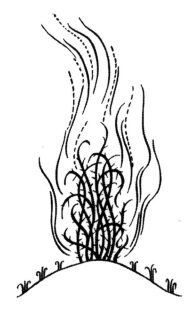

The Burning Bush.
Drawn by Rudolf Koch. Courtesy of Arion Press.

*****

Worldwide, lightning flashes about 30 to 100 times each second or about five million times per day. The accompanying sound of thunder roars. We might be scared by storms suddenly unleashing their energy with great light and sound. At the same time, we know that God's Power is beyond even the tremendous power in all the lightning bolts over the whole world because He, the Source of all, designed them.

In the book *The Shroud of Turin—An Adventure of Discovery* by Dr. and Mrs. Alan and Mary Whanger, we learn that recent scientific research indicates that a tremendous amount of energy at the Resurrection imaged Jesus and surrounding articles onto His burial Shroud. Dr. Bensen estimated that the electro-potential could have amounted to 100 million to as much as 200 million volts. Yet the energy release was focused and gentle, not destructive. Dr. Thaddeus Trenn called this a process of "weak dematerialization" whereby the subatomic particles overcame the strong nuclear bonds holding each atom together.

Warmth and light comfort us. Fireplaces and stoves warm homes in winter. Candles and electricity light the darkness. As the Chinese proverb and Christophers credo says, "It is better to light one candle than to curse the darkness." Fires can purify, changing rocky ore into useful and precious metals. We ask God to send the "fire of love" of His Holy Spirit to purify our hearts, minds, and souls. We trust in God's Divine Mercy. We consecrate ourselves to the source of Light, Life, and Truth, the Sacred Heart of Jesus through the Immaculate Heart of Mary.

*****

Exodus 19:16
On the morning of the third day there was thunder and lightning. A thick cloud covered the mountain, a loud trumpet blast was heard, and everyone in camp trembled with fear.

*****

Numbers 31:21–23
Eleazar then explained, "If you need to purify something that won't burn, such as gold, silver, bronze, iron, tin, or lead, you must first place it in a hot fire. After you take it out, sprinkle it with the water that purifies. Everything else should only be sprinkled with the water. Do all of this, just as the LORD commanded Moses."

*****

2 Samuel 22:13 (NIV)
Out of the brightness of his presence bolts of lightning blazed forth.

*****

Job 36:30
And when God sends lightning, it can be seen at the bottom of the sea.

*****

Job 37:2–3
…when I hear the roaring voice of God in the thunder, and when I see his lightning flash across the sky.

*****

Job 37:15–16
Can you explain why lightning flashes at the orders of God who knows all things? Or how he hangs the clouds in empty space?

*****

Psalm 18:12
Hailstones and fiery coals lit up the sky in front of you.

*****

Psalm 29:7
The voice of the LORD
makes lightning flash…

*****

Psalm 77:18
Your thunder roared
like chariot wheels.
The world was made bright
by lightning,
and all the earth trembled.

*****

Psalm 97:4
…and his lightning is so bright
that the earth sees it
and trembles.

*****

Psalm 135:7
The LORD makes the clouds rise
from far across the earth,
and he makes lightning
to go with the rain.
Then from his secret place
he sends out the wind.

*****

Ezekiel 1:4
I saw a windstorm blowing in from the north. Lightning flashed from a huge cloud and lit up the whole sky with a dazzling brightness. The fiery center of the cloud was as shiny as polished metal…

*****

Ezekiel 1:13–14
The creatures were glowing like hot coals, and I saw something like a flaming torch moving back and forth among them. Lightning flashed from the torch every time its flame blazed up. The creatures themselves moved as quickly as sparks jumping from a fire.

*****

Ezekiel 8:2
…and I saw something in the shape of a human. This figure was like fire from the waist down, and it was bright as polished metal from the waist up.

*****

Daniel 10:6
His body was like a precious stone, his face like lightning, his eyes like flaming fires, his arms and legs like polished bronze, and his voice like the roar of a crowd.

*****

Zechariah 9:14
Like a cloud, the LORD God will appear over his people, and his arrows will flash like lightning. God will sound his trumpet and attack in a whirlwind from the south.

*****

Matthew 24:27
The coming of the Son of Man will be like lightning that can be seen from east to west.

*****

Matthew 28:3
The angel looked as bright as lightning, and his clothes were white as snow.

*****

Luke 9:29 (NIV)
As he was praying, the appearance of his face changed, and his clothes became as bright as a flash of lightning.

*****

Luke 24:4 (NIV)
While they were wondering about this, suddenly two men in clothes that gleamed like lightning stood beside them.

*****

Revelation 4:5
Flashes of lightning and roars of thunder came out from the throne

in the center of the circle. Seven torches, which are the seven spirits of God, were burning in front of the throne.

*****

Revelation 8:5
After this, the angel filled the incense container with fire from the altar and threw it on the earth. Thunder roared, lightning flashed, and the earth shook.

*****

As fire refines gold, so suffering refines virtue.
—Chinese proverb.

*****

When the cross blue lightning seemed to open
The breast of heaven, I did present myself
Even in the aim and very flash of it.
—William Shakespeare (1564–1616). *Cassius, in Julius Caesar*, act 1, sc. 3, l. 50–2.

*****

The fire is the main comfort of the camp, whether in summer or winter, and is about as ample at one season as at another. It is as well for cheerfulness as for warmth and dryness.
—Henry David Thoreau. *"Ktaadn"* [1848], in *The Maine Woods* [1864], in *The Writings of Henry David Thoreau*, vol. 3, p. 43, Houghton Mifflin (1906).

*****

I saw the lightning's gleaming rod
Reach forth and write upon the sky
The awful autograph of God.
—Joaquin (Cincinnatus Hiner) Miller (1839?–1913). *The Ship in the Desert.*

*****

May sparks from the Holy Spirit "enkindle in us the fire of His Love." May the embers glow and warm our hearts and purify our souls. May our minds be enlightened with the knowledge of God's Love and the Gifts of the Holy Spirit. With the help and prayers of our Blessed Mother and all the saints and angels, may our good deeds warm the hearts and minds of others.

Aware of the dangers of lightning strikes and fires, it is important to educate one another about storms, fire safety and prevention. May land managers apply the principles learned from fire ecology such as prescribing controlled burns. We pray for victims of storms and fires, and for firefighters and rescue workers that God's angels may guide them in their mission to save life and property.

13

Flora

The Lily. The symbol of the Virgin Mary.
Drawn by Rudolf Koch. Courtesy of Arion Press.

*****

The flora encompasses an amazing array of life forms from algae, fungi, mushrooms and lichens, from tiny floating plants to herbs, shrubs and vines, to colossal trees. About 300,000 species of vascular plants grow upon this earth, with leaves, flowers, and fruits of varying shape, size, and color.

The color green reminds us of the shamrock that St. Patrick used to teach the Irish people about the Holy Trinity, three leaflets in one leaf, three Persons in one God. Jesus is the Good Shepherd who leads us to green pastures. He is the Vine and we are the branches. May we cooperate with divine grace, share in His Life abundantly, and bear good fruit.

As colorful flowers bloom and spread their color and fragrance over the earth, may we cultivate our talents and gifts to do the work God has created us to do and to share with those in need. May the Word of God find fertile soil within our hearts and may we cultivate our souls that we may yield a good harvest of life and goodness. May God inspire us so that our work can become a prayer. May we build up the Kingdom of God, as the seed that grows into the tree to shelter many birds. How wonderful is our God who provided us with plants for food, shelter, clothing, and medicine.

*****

Genesis 8:11
It (the dove) returned in the evening, holding in its beak a green leaf from an olive tree. Noah knew that the water was finally going down.

*****

Genesis 40:9–10
The king's personal servant told Joseph, "In my dream I saw a vine with three branches. As soon as it budded, it blossomed, and its grapes became ripe…"

*****

Exodus 2:3
But when she could no longer keep him hidden, she made a basket out of reeds and covered it with tar. She put him in the basket and placed it in the tall grass along the edge of the Nile River.

*****

Exodus 3:2
There an angel of the LORD appeared to him from a burning

bush. Moses saw that the bush was on fire, but it was not burning up.

*****

Numbers 17: 8
The next day when Moses went into the tent, flowers and almonds were already growing on Aaron's stick.

*****

Numbers 24:6
It's like a grove of palm trees or a garden beside a river. You are like tall aloe trees that the LORD has planted, or like cedars growing near water.

*****

Judges 9:8–15
Once the trees searched for someone to be king; they asked the olive tree, "Will you be our king?" But the olive tree replied, "My oil brings honor to people and gods. I won't stop making oil, just to have my branches wave above the other trees." Then they asked the fig tree, "Will you be our king?" But the fig tree replied, "I won't stop growing my delicious fruit, just to have my branches wave above the other trees." Next they asked the grape vine, "Will you be our king?" But the grape vine replied, "My wine brings cheer to people and gods. I won't stop making wine, just to have my branches wave above the other trees." Finally, they went to the thornbush and asked, "Will you be our king?" The thornbush replied, "If you really want me to be your king, then come into my shade and I will protect you. But if you're deceiving me, I'll start a fire that will spread out and destroy the cedars of Lebanon."

*****

1 Chronicles 16:33
Then every tree in the forest will sing joyful songs to the LORD. He is coming to judge all people on earth.

*****

Psalm 72:16 (NIV)
Let grain abound throughout the land;
on the tops of the hills may it sway.
Let its fruit flourish like Lebanon;
let it thrive like the grass of the field.

*****

Psalm 96:12
...and the fields to rejoice
with all of their crops.
Then every tree in the forest
will sing joyful songs...

*****

Ecclesiastes 2:5–6
I had flower gardens and orchards full of fruit trees. And I had
pools where I could get water for the trees.

*****

Song of Solomon 1:14
...you are flower blossoms from the gardens of En-Gedi.

*****

Song of Solomon 2:1
She Speaks:
I am merely a rose
from the land of Sharon,
a lily from the valley.

*****

Song of Solomon 4:13–14
Your arms are vines, covered with delicious fruits and all sorts of
spices—henna, nard, saffron, calamus, cinnamon, frankincense,
myrrh, and aloes—all the finest spices.

*****

Song of Solomon 6:11
I went down to see if blossoms were on the walnut trees, grape-vines, and fruit trees.

*****

Isaiah 11:1 (NIV)
A shoot will come up from the stump of Jesse; from his roots a Branch will bear fruit.

*****

Isaiah 27:6 (NIV)
In days to come Jacob will take root, Israel will bud and blossom and fill all the world with fruit.

*****

Isaiah 35:1
Thirsty deserts will be glad; barren lands will celebrate and blossom with flowers.

*****

Isaiah 41:19
I will fill the desert with all kinds of trees—cedars, acacias, and myrtles; olive and cypress trees; fir trees and pines.

*****

Isaiah 44:14
Either cedar, cypress, oak, or any tree from the forest may be cho-sen. Or even a pine tree planted by the woodcarver and watered by the rain.

*****

Isaiah 60:13
Wood from Lebanon's best trees will be brought to you—the pines, the firs, and the cypress trees. It will be used in my temple to make beautiful the place where I rest my feet.

*****

Ezekiel 17:23
All kinds of birds will find shelter under the tree, and they will rest in the shade of its branches.

*****

Ezekiel 31:3–9
There was once a cedar tree in Lebanon with large, strong branches reaching to the sky. This tree had plenty of water to help it grow tall, and nearby streams watered the other trees in the forest. But this tree towered over those other trees, and its branches grew long and thick. Birds built nests in its branches, and animals were born beneath it. People from all nations lived in the shade of this strong tree. It had beautiful, long branches, and its roots found water deep in the soil. None of the cedar trees in my garden of Eden were as beautiful as this tree; no tree of any kind had such long branches. I, the LORD, gave this tree its beauty, and I helped the branches grow strong. All other trees in Eden wanted to be just like it.

*****

Ezekiel 36:8
Trees will grow on you mountains of Israel and produce fruit for my people, because they will soon come home.

*****

Ezekiel 47:12
Fruit trees will grow all along this river and produce fresh fruit every month. The leaves will never dry out, because they will always have water from the stream that flows from the temple, and they will be used for healing people.

*****

Daniel 4:12
It was covered with leaves and heavy with fruit—enough for all nations. Wild animals enjoyed its shade, birds nested in its branches, and all creatures on earth lived on its fruit.

*****

Jonah 4:6–7, 10

The LORD made a vine grow up to shade Jonah's head and protect him from the sun. Jonah was very happy to have the vine, but early the next morning the LORD sent a worm to chew on the vine, and the vine dried up.…But the LORD said: You are concerned about a vine that you did not plant or take care of, a vine that grew up in one night and died the next.

*****

Micah 4:4

Everyone will find rest beneath their own fig trees or grape vines, and they will live in peace. This is a solemn promise of the LORD All-Powerful.

*****

Zechariah 8:12

Instead, I will make sure that your crops are planted in peace and your vineyards are fruitful, that your fields are fertile and the dew falls from the sky.

*****

Zechariah 11:2

Cry, you cyprus trees! The glorious cedars have fallen and are rotting. Cry, you oak trees of Bashan! The dense forest has been chopped down.

*****

Matthew 2:11

When the men went into the house and saw the child with Mary, his mother, they knelt down and worshiped him. They took out their gifts of gold, frankincense, and myrrh and gave them to him.

*****

Matthew 3:10
An ax is ready to cut the trees down at their roots. Any tree that doesn't produce good fruit will be chopped down and thrown into a fire.

*****

Matthew 13:32
Although it is the smallest of all seeds, it grows larger than any garden plant and becomes a tree. Birds even come and nest on its branches.

*****

Matthew 21:8
Many people spread clothes in the road, while others put down branches which they had cut from trees.

*****

Luke 12:27
Look how the wild flowers grow! They don't work hard to make their clothes. But I tell you that Solomon with all his wealth wasn't as well clothed as one of these flowers.

*****

Luke 17:6
Jesus replied: If you had faith no bigger than a tiny mustard seed, you could tell this mulberry tree to pull itself up, roots and all, and to plant itself in the ocean. And it would!

*****

Luke 21:29–31
Then Jesus told them a story: When you see a fig tree or any other tree putting out leaves, you know that summer will soon come. So, when you see these things happening, you know that God's kingdom will soon be here.

*****

John 12:13 (NIV)
They took palm branches and went out to meet him, shouting, "Hosanna!" "Blessed is he who comes in the name of the Lord!" "Blessed is the King of Israel!"

*****

John 15:1, 5
Jesus said to his disciples: I am the true vine, and my Father is the gardener....I am the vine, and you are the branches. If you stay joined to me, and I stay joined to you, then you will produce lots of fruit. But you cannot do anything without me.

*****

John 19:39
Nicodemus also came with about seventy-five pounds of spices made from myrrh and aloes. This was the same Nicodemus who had visited Jesus one night.

*****

Zechariah 4:3
One olive tree is on the right side and another on the left of the oil container.

*****

Revelation 11:4
These two witnesses are the two olive trees and the two lampstands that stand in the presence of the Lord who rules the earth.

*****

Revelation 22:2
Then it flowed down the middle of the city's main street. On each side of the river are trees that grow a different kind of fruit each month of the year. The fruit gives life, and the leaves are used as medicine to heal the nations.

*****

You will find something more in woods than in books. Trees and stones will teach you that which you can never learn from masters.
—St. Bernard (1090–1153), *Epistle* 106.

*****

There's not a plant or flower below,
but makes Thy glories known...
—Isaac Watts. *I Sing the Mighty Power of God* (*Praise for Creation and Providence*) [1715].

*****

Flowers laugh before thee upon their beds
And fragrance in thy footing treads;
Thou dost preserve the stars from wrong;
And the most ancient heavens, through thee, are fresh and strong.
—William Wordsworth. *Ode to Duty* (l. 45–48).

*****

Flowers have spoken to me more than I can tell in written words. They are the hieroglyphics of angels, loved by all men for the beauty of the character, though few can decypher even fragments of their meaning.
—Lydia M. Child (1802–1880). Letter: 1 September 1842. *Letters from New York, vol. 1, letter 26* [1843].

*****

Flowers...are a proud assertion that a ray of beauty outvalues all the utilities of the world.
—Ralph Waldo Emerson (1803–1882). *"Gifts," Essays, Second Series* [1844].

*****

Through basic and applied sciences at universities, botanical gardens, arboretums, forests, and herbaria, may we better study plants and fungi and their environments so as to develop a better understanding of their growth and survival, and ours too. May God inspire people to rediscover and share knowledge of plant use for food and medicine. Do we ever pause to recall where each dish at the table comes from? Food can be better transported to those who are hungry in the world. Facilities in developing countries could be improved to preserve and store surplus harvests. Do we contribute to feeding the poor and hungry? Do we provide them with the means to cultivate land and grow crops, and raise fish or farm animals? How can we better provide medicine and proper health care to the sick wherever they are in our world including the poorest nations? In turn, we can learn more about native and traditional food and medicinal uses of plants. Ecological tourism can provide a livelihood for developing societies.

Pressed flower of *Anemone coronaria* L. from the Holy Land:
(collector: J. E. Dimsmore 339, 2339 (Gray Herbarium), Jerusalem,
31 January 1903). Flowers of this species were identified on
photographs of the Shroud of Turin (see Danin, A. et al. 1999).

14

Fauna

Amazing is the diversity of living creatures from the microscopic protozoa to huge elephants and whales. There are two million to 15 million species of animals including between one and ten million species of insects. Children are fascinated by the stories of Noah's Ark, Jonah and the whale, Daniel in the lions' den. Children of all ages enjoy visiting zoos, aquariums, national parks, and wildlife refuges. St. Francis of Assisi preached to the birds, and St. Anthony of Padua preached to the fishes when others would not listen. May humankind help maintain the habitats where the fauna live, and remember our place sharing in their ecosystems and the biosphere at large. Because of our unique gift of the soul, humans should act wisely in taking care of the creatures entrusted to us.

Jesus is the Good Shepherd and we are His sheep. We form His flock, His faithful people the Church. May we always recognize His voice and follow Him to good pastures and restful waters. Together this flock is gathered by His representative, His vicar on earth, our Holy Father, the Pope. May God bless the Pope and all Bishops as they shepherd and guide us now. May they keep us safe from evil. May they lead the whole flock on the right path so that we may find good pastures and restful waters for our souls.

*****

1 Kings 4:33 (NIV)
He described plant life, from the cedar of Lebanon to the hyssop that grows out of walls. He also taught about animals and birds, reptiles and fish.

*****

Genesis 7: 1–3 (NIV)
The Lord then said to Noah, "Go into the ark, you and your whole family, because I have found you righteous in this generation. Take with you seven of every kind of clean animal, a male and its mate, and two of every kind of unclean animal, a male and its mate, and also seven of every kind of bird, male and female, to keep their various kinds alive throughout the earth…"

*****

Genesis 21:33
Abraham planted a tamarisk tree in Beersheba and worshiped the eternal LORD God.

*****

Daniel 6: 27
"…He rescues people and sets them free by working great miracles. Daniel's God has rescued him from the power of the lions."

*****

Isaiah 44:14
Either cedar, cypress, oak, or any tree from the forest may be chosen. Or even a pine tree planted by the woodcarver and watered by the rain.

*****

Job 12:8 (NIV)
…or speak to the earth, and it will teach you, or let the fish of the sea inform you.

*****

Psalm 8:8
...the birds in the sky,
the fish in the sea,
and all ocean creatures.

*****

Psalm 50:11
I know all the birds
in the mountains,
and every wild creature
is in my care.

*****

Psalm 76:4
You are more glorious than
the eternal mountains.

*****

Psalm 104:12
Birds build their nests nearby
and sing in the trees.

*****

Song of Solomon 2:12
flowers cover the earth,
it's time to sing.
The cooing of doves
is heard in our land.

*****

Jonah 1:17
The LORD sent a big fish to swallow Jonah, and Jonah was inside
the fish for three days and three nights.

*****

Matthew 3:4
John wore clothes made of camel's hair. He had a leather strap around his waist and ate grasshoppers and wild honey.

*****

Matthew 6:26
Look at the birds in the sky! They don't plant or harvest. They don't even store grain in barns. Yet your Father in heaven takes care of them. Aren't you worth more than birds?

*****

Matthew 10:16
Listen! I am sending you out just like sheep to a pack of wolves. You must be as cautious as snakes and as gentle as doves.

*****

Matthew 10:29-31
For only a penny you can buy two sparrows, yet not one sparrow falls to the ground without your Father's consent. As for you, even the hairs of your head have all been counted. So do not be afraid; you are worth much more than many sparrows!

*****

Matthew 13:47
The kingdom of heaven is like what happens when a net is thrown into a lake and catches all kinds of fish.

*****

Matthew 14:17, 19
But they said, "We have only five small loaves of bread and two fish."…and he told the crowd to sit down on the grass. Jesus took the five loaves and the two fish. He looked up toward heaven and blessed the food. Then he broke the bread and handed it to his disciples, and they gave it to the people.

*****

1 Corinthians 15:39
People, animals, birds, and fish are each made of flesh, but none of them are alike.

*****

Acts 10:12 (NIV)
It contained all kinds of fourfooted animals, as well as reptiles of the earth and birds of the air.

*****

Big fish eat small fish, and small fish eat shrimp eggs.
—Chinese proverb.

*****

O nightingale, that on yon bloomy spray
Warbl'st at eve, when all the woods are still.
—John Milton. *Sonnet, To the Nightingale* [c. 1637].

*****

Praise God, from whom all blessings flow!
Praise Him, all creatures here below!
Praise Him above, ye heavenly host!
Praise Father, Son, and Holy Ghost!
—Thomas Ken (1637–1711). *Doxology.* [1709].

*****

A man's interest in a single bluebird is worth more than a complete but dry list of the fauna and flora of a town.
—Henry David Thoreau. Letter, 22 November 1858, to Daniel Ricketson in *The Writings of Henry David Thoreau*, vol. 6, p. 341, Houghton Mifflin (1906).

*****

God's creativity and sense of humor are apparent in the existence and diversity of animals like the duckbill platypus, hummingbirds, kiwis and ostriches, seahorses, whales and dolphins. The fossil record allows us to peer into prehistory to witness the fascinating creatures that previously inhabited the earth—dinosaurs, pterosaurs, trilobites, saber-toothed tigers, and woolly mammoths. Museums remind us of more recently extinct animals like the dodo, moa, and passenger pigeon. Zoos remind us of the species threatened because of habitat loss. May we be careful not to cause another species extinction out of greed and senselessness.

Photo Credit: US National Oceanic and Atmospheric Administration.

15

Wings and Angels

People have always been fascinated by flight from butterflies and bees to birds and bats. Our eyes once again are raised to watch soaring wings and wonder about the view from up there. Passengers in airplanes and astronauts in space shuttles are awed by puffy clouds and icy seas and our smallness in relation to the earth below. Because wings seem to propel one closer to Heaven, another of God's creatures, angels have often been pictured as having wings. With the gift of these swift wings, angels can deliver messages from God and protect us from danger. May God bless our guardian angels as we greet one another.

*****

Genesis 7:14 (NIV)
They had with them every wild animal according to its kind, all livestock according to their kinds, every creature that moves along the ground according to its kind and every bird according to its kind, everything with wings.

*****

Exodus 19:4 (NIV)
You yourselves have seen what I did to Egypt, and how I carried you on eagles' wings and brought you to myself.

*****

Deuteronomy 32:11 (NIV)
…like an eagle that stirs up its nest and hovers over its young, that spreads its wings to catch them and carries them on its pinions.

*****

Ruth 2:12 (NIV)
May the Lord repay you for what you have done. May you be richly rewarded by the Lord, the God of Israel, under whose wings you have come to take refuge.

*****

Job 39:13
An ostrich proudly flaps her wings, but not because she loves her young.

*****

Job 39:26
Did you teach hawks to fly south for the winter?

*****

Psalm 17:8
Protect me as you would
your very own eyes;
hide me in the shadow
of your wings.

*****

Psalm 18:10
You rode on the backs
of flying creatures
and swooped down
with the wind as wings.

*****

Psalm 36:7
Your love is a treasure,
and everyone finds shelter
in the shadow of your wings.

*****

Psalm 55:6
I wish I had wings
like a dove,
so I could fly far away
and be at peace.

*****

Psalm 57:1
God Most High, have pity on me!
Have mercy.
I run to you
for safety.
In the shadow of your wings,
I seek protection
till danger dies down.

*****

Psalm 61:4
Let me live with you forever
and find protection
under your wings, my God.

*****

Psalm 63:7
You have helped me,
and I sing happy songs
in the shadow of your wings.

*****

Psalm 68:13
And for those who stayed back
to guard the sheep,
there are metal doves
with silver-coated wings
and shiny gold feathers.

*****

Psalm 91:4
He will spread his wings
over you
and keep you secure.
His faithfulness is like
a shield or a city wall.

*****

Psalm 104:3
…and you built your home
over the mighty ocean.
The clouds are your chariot
with the wind as its wings.

*****

Psalm 139:9
Suppose I had wings
like the dawning day
and flew across the ocean.

*****

Proverbs 23:5
Your money flies away
before you know it,
just like an eagle
suddenly taking off.

*****

Isaiah 6:2
Flaming creatures with six wings each were flying over him. They covered their faces with two of their wings and their bodies with two more. They used the other two wings for flying...

*****

Isaiah 8:8
Enemy soldiers will cover Judah like a flood reaching up to your neck. But God is with us. He will spread his wings and protect our land.

*****

Isaiah 34:15 (NIV)
The owl will nest there and lay eggs, she will hatch them, and care for her young under the shadow of her wings; there also the falcons will gather, each with its mate.

*****

Isaiah 40:31
But those who trust the LORD will find new strength. They will be strong like eagles soaring upward on wings; they will walk and run without getting tired.

*****

Ezekiel 1:5–6, 8–9, 11
...and in that center I saw what looked like four living creatures. They were somewhat like humans, except that each one had four faces and four wings. Under each of their wings, these creatures had a human hand. The four creatures were standing back to back with the tips of their wings touching. They moved together in every direction, without turning their bodies. Two wings of each creature were spread out and touched the wings of the creatures on either side. The other two wings of each creature were folded against its body.

*****

Ezekiel 1:22–25

Above the living creatures, I saw something that was sparkling like ice, and it reminded me of a dome. Each creature had two of its wings stretched out toward the creatures on either side, with the other two wings folded against its body. Whenever the creatures flew, their wings roared like an ocean or a large army or even the voice of God All-Powerful. And whenever the creatures stopped, they folded their wings against their bodies. When the creatures stopped flapping their wings, I heard a sound coming from above the dome.

*****

Ezekiel 3:13

It was the sound made by the creatures' wings as they brushed against each other, and by the rumble of the wheels beside them.

*****

Ezekiel 10:3, 5–21

The winged creatures were standing south of the temple when the man walked among them. A cloud filled the inner courtyard…The sound of the creatures' wings was as loud as the voice of God All-Powerful and could even be heard in the outer courtyard. The man in the robe was now standing beside a wheel. One of the four creatures reached its hand into the fire among them and gave him some of the hot coals. The man took the coals and left. I noticed again that each of the four winged creatures had what looked like human hands under their wings, and I saw the four wheels near the creatures. These wheels were shining like chrysolite. Each wheel was exactly the same and had a second wheel that cut through the middle of it, so that they could move in any direction without turning. The wheels moved together whenever the creatures moved. I also noticed that the wheels and the creatures' bodies, including their backs, their hands, and their wings, were covered with eyes. And I heard a voice calling these "the wheels that spin." Each of the winged creatures had four faces: the face of a bull, the face of a human, the face of a lion, and the face of an eagle. These were the same creatures I had seen near the Chebar River. They controlled when and where the wheels moved—the wheels went wherever the creatures went and stopped whenever they stopped. Even when the creatures flew in the air, the wheels stayed beside them. Then I watched the brightness of the LORD's glory move from the entrance of the temple and stop above the winged creatures. They spread their wings and flew into the air with the wheels at their side. They stopped at the east gate of the temple, and the LORD's glory was above them. They had four wings with hands beneath them, and they had the same four faces as those near the River. Each creature moved straight ahead without turning.

*****

Ezekiel 17:3, 7
…so they will understand what I am saying to them: A large eagle with strong wings and beautiful feathers once flew to Lebanon. It broke the top branch off a cedar tree, then carried it to a nation of merchants and left it in one of their cities. The eagle also took seed from Israel and planted it in a fertile field with plenty of water, like a willow tree beside a stream. The seed sprouted and grew into a grapevine that spread over the ground. It had lots of leaves and strong, deep roots, and its branches grew upward toward the eagle.

*****

Zechariah 5:9 (NIV)
Then I looked up—and there before me were two women, with the wind in their wings! They had wings like those of a stork, and they lifted up the basket between heaven and earth.

*****

Malachi 4:2 (NIV)
But for you who revere my name, the sun of righteousness will rise with healing in its wings. And you will go out and leap like calves released from the stall.

*****

Luke 13:34

Jerusalem, Jerusalem! Your people have killed the prophets and have stoned the messengers who were sent to you. I have often wanted to gather your people, as a hen gathers her chicks under her wings. But you wouldn't let me.

*****

Revelation 4:8

Each of the four living creatures had six wings, and their bodies were covered with eyes. Day and night they never stopped singing, "Holy, holy, holy is the Lord, the all-powerful God, who was and is and is coming!"

*****

Revelation 9:9

On their chests they wore armor made of iron. Their wings roared like an army of horse-drawn chariots rushing into battle.

*****

Revelation 12:14 (NIV)

The woman was given the two wings of a great eagle, so that she might fly to the place prepared for her in the desert, where she would be taken care of for a time, times and half a time, out of the serpent's reach.

*****

Hark! The herald angels sing
Glory to the newborn King…
With th'angelic host proclaim
Christ is born in Bethlehem.
—Charles Wesley (1707–1788). *Hymns and Sacred Poems* [1753], *Christmas Hymn: Hark! the Herald Angels Sing.*

*****

It came upon the midnight clear,
That glorious song of old,

From angels bending near the earth
To touch their harps of gold;
"Peace on the earth, good will to men
From heav'n's all-gracious King."
The world in solemn stillness lay
To hear the angels sing.
—Edmund Hamilton Sears (1810–1876). *The Angel's Song* [1850],
st. 1.

*****

…morning, at the brown brink eastward, springs—
Because the Holy Ghost over the bent
World broods with warm breast and with ah! bright wings.
—Gerard Manley Hopkins (1844–1889). *God's Grandeur* (l. 12–
14).

*****

Angel of God,
my Guardian dear,
to whom His love
commits me here,
ever this day (or night)
be at my side,
to light and guard,
to rule and guide.
Amen.
—Guardian Angel Prayer. A well-known prayer.

*****

St. Michael the Archangel, defend us in battle, be our protection
against the wickedness and snares of the Devil; may God rebuke
him, we humbly pray; and do thou, O Prince of the Heavenly
Host, by the Power of God, thrust into hell Satan and all the evil
spirits who prowl throughout the world seeking the ruin of souls.
Amen.
—Prayer attributed to Pope Leo XIII (1888).

Photo Credit: US National Oceanic and Atmospheric Administration.

16

The Human Family

"I am the Vine, ye are the branches."
Drawn by Rudolf Koch. Courtesy of Arion Press.

*****

About two million years after the time of our first parents "Adam and Eve", about six billion people now inhabit the earth, and God loves every one of us uniquely and together. May we see each human person as a precious child, a "temple of the Holy Spirit" (1 Cor 6:19), "created in the image and likeness of God" (Gen 1:26). May we respect human life from the moment of conception until natural death. May we allow Christ to live in us. May we see one another with the eyes of Jesus, listen to one another with His ears, and help one another with His hands.

How wonderful is the human family living in harmony, our children "like olive plants around our table" (Ps 128:3). May God bless all families, husbands and wives, fathers and mothers, children, the young, middle-aged, and the elderly with the fruits of the Holy Spirit: love, joy, peace, kindness, goodness, humility, and self control (Gal 5:22). May we mirror the love of the Holy Family. The family is a nucleus for the larger Church, each home a sacred chapel united within a worldwide cathedral. May our prayers rise up and join that of all families, for forgiveness, justice and peace in our hearts and in the world, and renewed family and Church life today.

Together as the Church, our families build up the community. We experience communion within the community, within our Church, home, school, workplace, city, country, and the world. We stand together in wonder and awe in the Presence of God. Here we are on one side of the ocean looking at the same body of water that our brothers and sisters are seeing from the other side. A 12th grade religion class in Liberia prized the following as community values: love, care, cooperation, unity, respect, friendship, happiness, family, hospitality, sharing, kindness, education, and tradition (St. Martin's, Gbarnga, Liberia, July 1985). When we live simply, we can more readily share.

Jesus gave us a mission, to "go out to all the world and tell the Good News" (Mk 16:15). Jesus called the first apostles to be "fishers of men" (Mk 1:17). He recognized that "the harvest is rich but the laborers are few" (Lk 10:2). We pray for vocations to the priesthood and religious life, for missionaries and teachers. We pray for them that they may be completely dedicated to Christ and His Church. May God bless them with the gifts necessary to live by the evangelical counsels of poverty, chastity, and obedience. Let us remember to thank the priests, brothers, and sisters who serve and pray for us.

How do all of us tell the good news? Many around us simply need a little encouragement, a prayer, a kind word, and our example so that they can cross the threshold to faith and to the Church. "Now is the acceptable time, now is the day of salvation" (2 Cor 6:2). As "citizens of Heaven" (Phil 3:20), let us remind one another about God's Love for us. May we share the gifts, talents, and resources that we have with one another. As Mother Teresa of Calcutta said, "In this life we cannot do great things. We can only do small things with great love." So let us do every small thing for the love of God. May we pray and work for peace, understanding, forgiveness, and reconciliation in our own families and around the world. In the Eucharist—in Holy Communion, we are together in Christ. "We are one body in Christ" (Rom 12:5, 1 Cor 12:27, Col 3:15).

*****

Genesis 2:24 (NIV)
For this reason a man will leave his father and mother and be united to his wife, and they will become one flesh.

*****

Exodus 20:12 (NIV)
Honor your father and your mother, so that you may live long in the land the Lord your God is giving you.

*****

Proverbs 1:8
My child, obey the teachings
of your parents…

*****

Proverbs 27:27
From the milk of the goats, you can make enough cheese to feed your family and all your servants.

*****

Proverbs 31:15
She gets up before daylight to prepare food for her family and for her servants.

*****

Song of Solomon 4:16
She Speaks:
Let the north wind blow,
the south wind too!
Let them spread the aroma
of my garden,
so the one I love
may enter
and taste
its delicious fruits.

*****

Matthew 10:42
And anyone who gives one of my most humble followers a cup of cool water, just because that person is my follower, will surely be rewarded.

*****

Matthew 19:29
All who have given up home or brothers and sisters or father and mother or children or land for me will be given a hundred times as much. They will also have eternal life.

*****

Mark 5:19
But Jesus would not let him. Instead, he said, "Go home to your family and tell them how much the Lord has done for you and how good he has been to you."

*****

Mark 5:41 (NIV)
After he put them all out, he took the child's father and mother and the disciples who were with him, and went in where the child was. He took her by the hand and said to her, "Talitha koum!" (which means, "Little girl, I say to you, get up!").

*****

Luke 2:33 (NIV)
The child's father and mother marveled at what was said about him.

*****

Acts 10:2
Cornelius was a very religious man. He worshiped God, and so did everyone else who lived in his house. He had given a lot of money to the poor and was always praying to God.

*****

Acts 28:2
The local people were very friendly, and they welcomed us by building a fire, because it was rainy and cold.

*****

1 Timothy 5:4
But if a widow has children or grandchildren, they should learn to serve God by taking care of her, as she once took care of them. This is what God wants them to do.

*****

Hebrews 11:7
Because Noah had faith, he was warned about something that had not yet happened. He obeyed and built a boat that saved him and his family. In this way the people of the world were judged, and Noah was given the blessings that come to everyone who pleases God.

*****

1 Corinthians 7:3–4 (NIV)
The husband should fulfill his marital duty to his wife, and likewise the wife to her husband. The wife's body does not belong to her alone but also to her husband. In the same way, the husband's body does not belong to him alone but also to his wife.

*****

Ephesians 5:23, 28, 33
A husband is the head of his wife, as Christ is the head and the Savior of the church, which is his own body. In the same way, a husband should love his wife as much as he loves himself. A husband who loves his wife shows that he loves himself. So each husband should love his wife as much as he loves himself, and each wife should respect her husband.

*****

Galatians 5:22 (NIV)
But the fruit of the Spirit is love, joy, peace, patience, kindness, goodness, faithfulness…

*****

1 Peter 3:8
Finally, all of you should agree and have concern and love for each other. You should also be kind and humble.

*****

Revelation 7:9
After this, I saw a large crowd with more people than could be counted. They were from every race, tribe, nation, and language, and they stood before the throne and before the Lamb. They wore white robes and held palm branches in their hands…

*****

No man is an island entire of itself. Each is a piece of the continent, a part of the main.
—John Donne (1572–1631).

*****

Man is but a reed, the weakest in nature, but he is a thinking reed.
—Blaise Pascal. *Pensées* [1670], 347.

*****

Live Jesus in our hearts, forever.
—Bl. Edmund Ignatius Rice, CFC (1762–1844). Concluding prayer regularly repeated throughout the day by the Congregation of Christian Brothers.

*****

The height of a creature's love returning to God is the Immaculata—a being without stain of sin, wholly beautiful, wholly belonging to God. Not even for a moment did her will bend away from the will of God....When, O Mother Immaculate, will you become queen of all and each soul in particular? When will all the souls in the entire world know the goodness and love of your heart toward them?
—St. Maximilian Kolbe. *Aim Higher!: Spiritual and Marian reflections of St. Maximilian Kolbe.* Prow Books / Franciscan Marytown Press.

*****

Look with hope to the future and welcome with trust the challenges of the third millennium, fully aware that Christ is by your sides. You, who by virtue of your charism, are particularly called to revive the faith and rekindle the fire of charity in all circumstances, are invited to clearly keep the preferential option for the 'image of God', which is waiting to be revealed in the lives of every brother and sister. Learn to recognize the face of Christ in every person.
—Pope John Paul II, 6 October 1998 (VIS—Vatican Information Service). With permission.

*****

During the days of creation, God looked at His handiwork and saw that what He made was good. It could not be otherwise. The harmony of nature reflected the perfection of the Creator. Finally, God created man. He created him in His own image and likeness. He entrusted to him the magnificence of the world so that, by enjoying and using its goods in a free and rational way, he would cooperate actively in bringing God's work to perfection. When man sinned sin not only broke the bond of love between man and God...it also disturbed the harmony of all creation. If, however, the world shared in the effects of sin, it also shared in the divine promise of the Redemption when the Son of God came to embrace creation anew...to restore to creation its original holiness and dignity
—Pope John Paul II, 12 June 1999 (VIS—Vatican Information Service). With permission.

*****

I dream that people did not call names
Instead sit down and play some games
There would be absolutely no poor
Everyone would have a house with a dutch door
Everybody would have food
and nobody would be rude.
It may be hard to do
But someday I hope it will come true!
—Jonathan A. Brach (2001, the author's son at 10 yr. old). With Permission.

*****

To see the face of God
In one another
To touch the hand of God
As we help a child take first steps
And help a senior from a chair
To hear the laughter of God

In the young and old
To breathe the breath of God
Upon the wind
To taste the sweetness of God
From the food He provides
And in the Bread of Life
To be embraced by the hug of God
Through a parent or spouse
To be bathed in the shower of God
By every shower and dew
And in Baptismal waters
To shine in the radiance of God
To reflect that light to all.
Filled with the Spirit of God,
To live the Love of God.
—Anthony R. Brach (1985).

The author's family (2000).

17

Servants and Co-Creators

The Washing of Feet.
Drawn by Rudolf Koch. Courtesy of Arion Press.

*****

We can learn about true stewardship and co-creation from the Bible. We are called to first appreciate God's gifts in creation. Then with grateful thanks, we can be better stewards (servants) and "caretakers" (Gen 2:15). We need to "take care" of our families, communities, homes, and the earth. The people of the Bible tell us about God and life from their experience living close to the land and sea as shepherds, farmers, fishermen, and as members of families and tribes. Shepherds guided their sheep to new pastures and fresh water. They guarded their flocks. Jesus is the Good Shepherd who leads us. Farmers plowed, planted, fertilized, cultivated, weeded, and harvested the fields. God plants the seed of faith, hope, and love in our hearts. Fishermen repaired nets and spent long days fishing from their boats. Jesus called his apostles to be fishers of men, to gather other persons to follow Him. Parents raised their children and leaders took care of their people.

God chose Abraham and led His people to the Promised Land where they learned how to take care of the land for farming and how to fish in the sea. During their Exodus from captivity in Egypt, the Israelites survived in the desert. Although they wandered, Moses trusted in God Who provided them with water to drink, and manna and quails for food. John the Baptist lived on locusts and wild honey. Jesus fasted in the desert for 40 days. Jesus and his disciples walked many miles.

What about us? Do we trust in God's Providence? Are we grateful for our blessings of water, shelter, and food? What do we do to help others survive the elements and hunger? Do we "wash one another's feet" (Jn 13:14) by being charitable to those in our charge, our families and communities? Do we donate non-perishable food, clothing, and money? Do we make an effort to live close to the land? Do we walk and use public transportation when possible? Do we conserve water and energy? Do we support alternative forms of energy such as solar, wind, tidal, wave, hydroelectric, and geothermal power? Do we recycle paper, plastic, glass, and metal? Do we preserve natural habitats in the wilderness, and create gardens and parks in our cities? Do we take care of the land, sea, and the air, and the flora and fauna that depend upon them?

Do we cooperate with God's Plan for creation? Do we acknowledge the beauty of creation, and His own designs in nature? May we remember both the unitive and pro-creative aspects of marriage. May God bless our homes and families. May we be life-giving people. May we cherish life from the moment of conception until natural death. May all people realize that in-vitro fertilization, cloning, and embryonic stem cell research are wrong because tiny human lives are destroyed in the process. May we encourage adoption of children in need of homes and provide better care of our infirmed and aged seniors.

*****

Genesis 3:17–19
The LORD said to the man, "You listened to your wife and ate fruit from that tree. And so, the ground will be under a curse because of what you did. As long as you live, you will have to struggle to grow enough food. Your food will be plants, but the ground will produce thorns and thistles. You will have to sweat to earn a living; you were made out of soil, and you will once again turn into soil."

*****

Genesis 43:24
The servant took them into Joseph's house and gave them water to wash their feet. He also tended their donkeys.

*****

2 Samuel 17:28
Here is a list of what they brought: sleeping mats, blankets, bowls, pottery jars, wheat, barley, flour, roasted grain, beans, lentils, honey, yogurt, sheep, and cheese. They brought the food for David and the others because they knew that everyone would be hungry, tired, and thirsty from being out in the desert.

*****

Job 31:38
I have never mistreated the land I farmed and made it mourn.

*****

Isaiah 28:24
Farmers don't just plow and break up the ground.

*****

Amos 7:14
I answered: I'm not a prophet! And I wasn't trained to be a prophet. I am a shepherd, and I take care of fig trees.

*****

Matthew 13:3 (NIV)
Then he told them many things in parables, saying: "A farmer went out to sow his seed…"

*****

Matthew 13:24, 30 (NIV)
Jesus told them another parable: "The kingdom of heaven is like a man who sowed good seed in his field….Let both grow together until the harvest. At that time I will tell the harvesters: First collect the weeds and tie them in bundles to be burned; then gather the wheat and bring it into my barn."

*****

Mark 1:16
As Jesus was walking along the shore of Lake Galilee, he saw Simon and his brother Andrew. They were fishermen and were casting their nets into the lake.

*****

Luke 2:8
That night in the fields near Bethlehem some shepherds were guarding their sheep.

*****

Luke 12:17
…and he said to himself, "What can I do? I don't have a place large enough to store everything."

*****

Luke 13:8
The gardener answered, "Master, leave it for another year. I'll dig around it and put some manure on it to make it grow…"

*****

John 13:14
And if your Lord and teacher has washed your feet, you should do the same for each other.

*****

Acts 20:28 (NIV)
Keep watch over yourselves and all the flock of which the Holy Spirit has made you overseers. Be shepherds of the church of God, which he bought with his own blood.

*****

1 Timothy 5:10
She must also be well-known for doing all sorts of good things, such as raising children, giving food to strangers, welcoming God's people into her home, helping people in need, and always making herself useful.

*****

2 Timothy 2:6 (NIV)
The hardworking farmer should be the first to receive a share of the crops.

*****

James 5:7, 18
My friends, be patient until the Lord returns. Think of farmers who wait patiently for the spring and summer rains to make their valuable crops grow. But when he did pray for rain, it fell from the skies and made the crops grow.

*****

Dost thou wish to receive mercy?
Show mercy to thy neighbor.
—St. John Chrysostom (ca. 347–407), *Homily* XIII:7

*****

Oh, Adam was a gardener, and God who made him sees
That half a proper gardener's work is done upon his knees.
—Rudyard Kipling. *The Glory of the Garden* [1911], st. 8.

*****

The Knight of Immaculata does not confine his heart to himself, nor to his family, relatives, neighbors, friends, or countrymen, but embraces the whole world, each and every soul, because without exception, they have all been redeemed by the blood of Jesus.
—St. Maximilian Kolbe. *Aim Higher!: Spiritual and Marian reflections of St. Maximilian Kolbe.* Prow Books / Franciscan Marytown Press.

*****

...Who are we? Who is man? Who are we who are capable of so much? It is good for us also to reflect on progress. Today humanity's scientific and operative development has reached goals that seemed unattainable. How much further can man's thought and action go? Admiration, enthusiasm, a passion for instruments, for the products of man's intelligence and hands—all these fascinate us, perhaps to the point of madness. And herein lies the danger; we must be careful not to idolize these instruments. Undoubtedly they multiply man's efficiency beyond all limits, but is this efficiency always in his favor? Does it make him good? More a man? Or, perhaps, could these instruments not make man, who produces them, a prisoner and...a slave of the system of life the instruments impose on their master in their production and use? Man's heart must become even more free, more good, and more religious as the power of machines, arms, and the instruments man puts at his disposition grow greater and more dangerous.
—Pope Paul VI, 20 July 1969 (VIS—Vatican Information Service). With permission.

*****

Faced with the widespread destruction of the environment, people everywhere are coming to understand that we cannot continue to use the goods of the Earth as we have in the past...a new ecological awareness is beginning to emerge…The ecological crisis is a moral issue.

—Pope John Paul II, *The Ecological Crisis: A Common Responsibility*, nos. 1, 15, 8 December 1989 (VIS—Vatican Information Service). With permission.

*****

The rising concern for preservation of the environment is one of "signs of hope" which the Holy Spirit provides for our times. Today, mankind has discovered—largely in reaction to the indiscriminate exploitation of natural resources which has often accompanied industrial development—the significance and the value of an environment which remains a hospitable home for man, where mankind is destined to live. Environmental dangers forced world leaders in science, industry, and government to find new ways to use the earth's resources responsibly. The key challenge is not only to limit the damage which has already been done, and apply remedies, but especially to find approaches to development which are in harmony with respect and protection for the natural environment. For believers, preservation of the environment takes on a special importance insofar as the world is seen as the design of the Creator. Mankind was commissioned by God to act as steward for the earth's resources, and guardian of God's "creative work."

—Pope John Paul II, 18 November 1998 (VIS—Vatican Information Service). With permission.

*****

The promotion of human dignity is linked to the right to a healthy environment, since this right highlights the dynamics of the relationship between the individual and society. A body of international, regional and national norms on the environment is gradually giving juridic form to this right. But juridic measures by themselves are not sufficient. The danger of serious damage to land and sea, and to the climate, flora and fauna, calls for a profound change in modern civilization's typical consumer life-style, particularly in the richer countries. Nor can we underestimate another risk, even if it is a less drastic one: people who live in poverty in rural areas can be driven by necessity to exploit beyond sustainable limits the little land which they have at their disposal. Special training aimed at teaching them how to harmonize the cultivation of the land with respect for the environment needs to be encouraged. The world's present and future depend on the safeguarding of creation, because of the endless interdependence between human beings and their environment. Placing human well-being at the centre of concern for the environment is actually the surest way of safeguarding creation; this in fact stimulates the responsibility of the individual with regard to natural resources and their judicious use.

—Pope John Paul II, 8 December 1998. (VIS—Vatican Information Service). With permission.

*****

Everyone has the moral duty to preserve the environment and all of God's creation. We know that it is not just a matter of what is nowadays called ecology. It is not just enough to seek the cause of the world's destruction only in excessive industrialization, uncritical applications in industry and agriculture of scientific and technological advances, or in unbridled pursuit of wealth without concern for the future effects of all these actions. Although it cannot be denied that these actions do case great harm, it is easy to see that their source is deeper: It lies in man's very attitude. It appears that what is most dangerous for creation and for man is lack of respect for the laws of nature and the disappearance of a sense of the value of life. Is it really possible to oppose the destruction of the environment while allowing, in the name of comfort and convenience, the slaughter of the unborn and the procured death of the elderly and infirm, and the carrying out, in the name of progress, of unacceptable interventions and forms of experimentation at the very beginning of human life? When the good of science or economic interests prevail over the good of the person, and ultimately of whole societies, environmental destruction is a sign of a real contempt for man. All followers of Christ ought to examine their own life-style, to ensure that the legitimate pursuit of prosperity does not suppress the voice of conscience which judges what is right and what is truly good.

—Pope John Paul II, 12 June 1999 (VIS—Vatican Information Service). With permission.

*****

A human ecology will render the life of creatures more dignified, protecting the radical good of life in all its manifestations, and preparing an environment for future generations that is closer to the plan of the Creator....(Humankind's role in Genesis I)...is not the mission of an absolute and uncensurable master, but of a minister of the Kingdom of God, called to continue the work of the Creator, a work of life and peace. If one looks at the regions of our planet, one realizes immediately that humanity has disappointed the divine expectation. Man has unhesitatingly devastated wooded plains and valleys, polluted the waters, deformed the earth's habitat, made the air unbreathable, upset the hydrogeological and atmospheric systems, blighted green spaces, implemented uncontrolled forms of industrialization, humiliating—to use an image of Dante Alighieri—the earth, that flower-bed that is our dwelling. Given this situation, it is necessary to stimulate and support an ecological conversion, which over the last few decades has made humanity more sensitive when facing the catastrophe toward which it was moving. Not only is a physical ecology at stake, attentive to safeguarding the habitat of different living beings, but also a human ecology that will render the life of creatures more dignified. (Quoting a passage from the Jewish Hasidim tradition): "You are wherever I go! You are wherever I stop...wherever I turn, wherever I admire, only You, again You, always You."
—Pope John Paul II, 17 January 2001 (VIS—Vatican Information Service). With permission.

*****

This sentiment for a human ecology based on human solidarity was repeated in a Vatican Document in Preparation for a Summit on Sustainable Development (13 June 2002). Ecology is the study of interrelationships between organisms and their environment; thus, human ecology provides a way to understand how we interact with the earth and all of God's creatures that share this space with us. Because human society is founded upon the family, it is in the context of our families, that we learn about the goodness of God's gift to us of this earth and how we should respect and care for the world's resources, air, water, and land, flora, and fauna.

Archangel Raphael.
Drawn by Rudolf Koch. Courtesy of Arion Press.

18

Suffering

The Crown of Thorns.
Drawn by Rudolf Koch. Courtesy of Arion Press.

*****

Have natural disasters and tragic world events ever brought tears to your eyes? Is humankind bringing its own punishment upon itself? "Every action has a reaction..." Have you ever wondered about the Reality beyond both sorrowful times? Reflecting upon the sorrows encapsulated in the words of Holy Scripture moves us to compassion. The Word Himself comforts us in our trials and sufferings and sends His Holy Spirit to heal and strengthen us.

As Jesus tells us, "take up my yoke and learn from me for I am meek and humble of heart. And you'll find rest for your souls, for my yoke is easy, and my burden is light" (Mt 11:29). When we suffer, may we take up the wood of the Cross and to do His Will. We are called to take up our cross daily. Mother Teresa of Calcutta said that suffering is like "a kiss from God." God does not create the suffering to harm us but rather sometimes permits it so that a greater good may result. St. Peter reminds us that we may have for a time to suffer many trials but this is so that our faith which is more precious than gold, may be genuine and lead us to praise Jesus when He appears (1 Pt 1:7).

As we pray the Lord's Prayer, we say "Our Father Who art in Heaven…Your Kingdom come, your Will be done, on earth as it is in Heaven…" (Mt 6:9). May God's Will not mine be done. Or better yet, may our wills be transformed into that which God seeks. Then when asked, "were you there when they crucified my Lord?", we will be able to identify with our suffering Lord. As we pray the Chaplet of Divine Mercy (given to St. Sister M. Faustina Kowalska, 1905–1938), "by His most sorrowful passion, may God have mercy on us, and on the whole world." Thus may we comfort others as our lives, faith, hope, love, and joy have been restored.

What do we do to alleviate the pain and suffering in our world? To stop the wars and violence in the world, we need to change our own hearts first and to forgive one another from the heart. We can ask which of the corporal and spiritual works of mercy is God asking me to do at the present moment. May we pray for one another and be generous to the sick and those in need. Finally, may God grant abundant miracles of healing the suffering so that they may praise God and share their renewed life and faith with their families and friends.

*****

Psalm 137:1–2
Beside the rivers of Babylon we thought about Jerusalem, and we sat down and cried. We hung our small harps on the willow trees.

*****

Isaiah 38:17
It was for my own good that I had such hard times. But your love

protected me from doom in the deep pit, and you turned your eyes away from my sins.

*****

Habakkuk 3:17–18
Fig trees may no longer bloom, or vineyards produce grapes; olive trees may be fruitless, and harvest time a failure; sheep pens may be empty, and cattle stalls vacant—but I will still celebrate because the LORD God saves me.

*****

Mark 5:34
Jesus said to the woman, "You are now well because of your faith. May God give you peace! You are healed, and you will no longer be in pain."

*****

John 19:1–3, 16–18, 26–30
Pilate gave orders for Jesus to be beaten with a whip. The soldiers made a crown out of thorn branches and put it on Jesus. Then they put a purple robe on him. They came up to him and said, "Hey, you king of the Jews!" They also hit him with their fists.... Then Pilate handed Jesus over to be nailed to a cross. Jesus was taken away, and he carried his cross to a place known as "The Skull." In Aramaic this place is called "Golgotha." The place was probably given this name because it was near a large rock in the shape of a human skull. There Jesus was nailed to the cross, and on each side of him a man was also nailed to a cross.... When Jesus saw his mother and his favorite disciple with her, he said to his mother, "This man is now your son." Then he said to the disciple, "She is now your mother." From then on, that disciple took her into his own home. Jesus knew that he had now finished his work. And in order to make the Scriptures come true, he said, "I am thirsty!" A jar of cheap wine was there. Someone then soaked a sponge with the wine and held it up to Jesus' mouth on the stem of a hyssop plant. After Jesus drank the wine, he said, "Everything is done!" He bowed his head and died.

*****

2 Corinthians 1:7
You never disappoint us. You suffered as much as we did, and we know that you will be comforted as we were.

*****

1 Peter 1:6–7
On that day you will be glad, even if you have to go through many hard trials for a while. Your faith will be like gold that has been tested in a fire. And these trials will prove that your faith is worth much more than gold that can be destroyed. They will show that you will be given praise and honor and glory when Jesus Christ returns.

*****

1 Peter 4:19
If you suffer for obeying God, you must have complete faith in your faithful Creator and keep on doing right.

*****

1 Peter 5:9
But you must resist the devil and stay strong in your faith. You know that all over the world the Lord's followers are suffering just as you are.

*****

Revelation 2:10
Don't worry about what you will suffer. The devil will throw some of you into jail, and you will be tested and made to suffer for ten days. But if you are faithful until you die, I will reward you with a glorious life.

*****

Revelation 21:4
He will wipe all tears from their eyes, and there will be no more

death, suffering, crying, or pain. These things of the past are gone forever.

*****

Take Lord, receive all my liberty, my memory, understanding, my entire will. Give me only your Love and your Grace; that's enough for me. Your Love and your Grace are enough for me.
—St. Ignatius of Loyola (1491–1556). A well-known prayer.

*****

No Cross, No Crown.
—William Penn (1644–1718). *Title of pamphlet* [1669].

*****

When a storm strikes a ship out at sea, the ship does not stop, does not struggle, but peacefully sails onward. Similarly when the storm in our soul rages, we should not struggle, we should not lose our peace, but turn toward the Immaculata and then go forward with absolute confidence....Suffering for love nourishes love....Whoever is capable of suffering much for love can be happy that his love is deep....Spiritual joy is born of sacrifice.
—St. Maximilian Kolbe. *Aim Higher!: Spiritual and Marian reflections of St. Maximilian Kolbe.* Prow Books / Franciscan Marytown Press.

*****

...Striving with all our strength to correspond to the invitations of God's grace and increase his glory through the Immaculate Virgin in ourselves and in others, we sometimes experience the happy peace of a child who, having placed himself unreservedly into the hands of its mother, worries about nothing, fears nothing, ever trusting in the wisdom, goodness and strength of his mother. Sometimes it will happen that the tempest will be all-encompassing, lightning will strike and thunder will roar, but we who are totally in the hands of the Immaculata can be certain that nothing will harm us, as long as our heavenly Mother is with us and as long

as she does not will it.
—St. Maximilian Kolbe. *Will to Love—Reflections for Daily Living by St. Maximilian Kolbe, "Prophet of the Civilization of Love."* Marytown Press.

*****

As believers, how can we fail to see that abortion, euthanasia and assisted suicide are a terrible rejection of God's gift of life and love?
—Pope John Paul II (VIS—Vatican Information Service). With permission.

*****

Lord Jesus Christ, Son of the Father, send now Your Spirit over the earth. Let the Holy Spirit live in the hearts of all nations, that they may be preserved from degeneration, disasters and war. May the Lady of All Nations, who once was Mary, be our Advocate, Amen.
—Prayer attributed to Our Lady of All Nations given to visionary Ida Peerdeman on 11 February 1951. With permission of the Foundation "Lady of all Nations," Amsterdam.

Pressed thistle plant *Gundelia tournefortii* L.:
collectors: E. Weinert & A. Mousawi, without collection number
(Gray Herbarium), Adhaim, Iraq, 20 March 1973. The spiny leaves
of this plant were likely used in the "crown of thorns" placed upon
the head of Jesus (see Danin, A. et al. 1999).

19

Death and Resurrection

The Butterfly, a symbol of the Resurrection of the Body.
Drawn by Rudolf Koch. Courtesy of Arion Press.

*****

Sister death will meet us all at the end of our earthly life like a window or portal to eternal life. May our lives be worthy of eternal life with God in Heaven. "Death has no more power over Him" (Romans 6:9). "Death has been swallowed up in victory. Where, O death, is your victory? Where, O death, is your sting?" (1 Corinthians 15:54–55) "…Holy Mary, Mother of God, pray for us sinners, now and at the hour of our death. Amen." "Jesus and Mary, I love you. Save souls." Our faith is in the Risen Lord who will transform this earthly body of ours too in the Resurrection.

Alleluia! Our faith and hope are in the Resurrection of Jesus, God's only begotten Son. The Empty Tomb—He is Risen! Alleluia! May we meet Him in the garden like Mary Magdalene, and treasure His Presence in the Word and the Eucharist, and finally upon our death may we see His radiant Holy Face and hear Him call our name. The burial shroud of Our Lord recalls not only His passion and death but also His Resurrection on Easter morning. Images of the terrible instruments of His death and the loving flowers left surrounding His Body are imprinted upon the cloth, a sign of forgiveness and reconciliation. The Holy Face of our Risen Lord shines beyond the veil separating this world and the next. He sends us forth to teach all nations. He sends His Holy Spirit, the Advocate to remind us of all that He has told us.

The seed germinating and the caterpillar transforming into a butterfly, remind us of the transforming power of the Resurrection and new life. God wants us to share in His Life in Heaven after our earthly life. As the *Baltimore Catechism* taught, "God made us to know Him, to love Him, and to serve Him in this world so as to be forever happy with him in the next." We pray for our departed brothers and sisters so that they may share in that Life, and that we may rejoice with them too in Heaven someday. We look forward to restoration and renewal. Humankind awaits the Parousia, the Second Coming of Jesus. We do not know the day or the hour but we joyfully await Him whether it is soon or millennia from now. "There will be a new Heavens and a new earth" (Is 65:17, Rev 21:1). There will be no more sadness or pain for all will rejoice in God's eternal home. "Maranatha—Come Lord Jesus" (Rev 22:20).

*****

Isaiah 26:19
Your people will rise to life! Tell them to leave their graves and celebrate with shouts. You refresh the earth like morning dew; you give life to the dead.

*****

Ezekiel 37:1–7 (NIV)
The hand of the LORD was upon me, and he brought me out by

the Spirit of the LORD and set me in the middle of a valley; it was full of bones. He led me back and forth among them, and I saw a great many bones on the floor of the valley, bones that were very dry. He asked me, "Son of man, can these bones live?" I said, "O Sovereign LORD, you alone know." Then he said to me, "Prophesy to these bones and say to them, 'Dry bones, hear the word of the LORD! This is what the Sovereign LORD says to these bones: I will make breath enter you, and you will come to life. I will attach tendons to you and make flesh come upon you and cover you with skin; I will put breath in you, and you will come to life. Then you will know that I am the LORD.'" So I prophesied as I was commanded. And as I was prophesying, there was a noise, a rattling sound, and the bones came together, bone to bone.

*****

John 11:25 (NIV)
Jesus said to her, "I am the resurrection and the life. He who believes in me will live, even though he dies…"

*****

Romans 8:18–23 (NIV)
I consider that our present sufferings are not worth comparing with the glory that will be revealed in us. The creation waits in eager expectation for the sons of God to be revealed. For the creation was subjected to frustration, not by its own choice, but by the will of the one who subjected it, in hope that the creation itself will be liberated from its bondage to decay and brought into the glorious freedom of the children of God. We know that the whole creation has been groaning as in the pains of childbirth right up to the present time. Not only so, but we ourselves, who have the firstfruits of the Spirit, groan inwardly as we wait eagerly for our adoption as sons, the redemption of our bodies.

*****

1 Corinthians 15:21, 42 (NIV)
For since death came through a man, the resurrection of the dead comes also through a man.…So will it be with the resurrection of

the dead. The body that is sown is perishable, it is raised imperishable...

*****

1 Peter 1:3 (NIV)
Praise be to the God and Father of our Lord Jesus Christ! In his great mercy he has given us new birth into a living hope through the resurrection of Jesus Christ from the dead...

*****

1 Peter 3:21
Those flood waters were like baptism that now saves you. But baptism is more than just washing your body. It means turning to God with a clear conscience, because Jesus Christ was raised from death.

*****

At the moment of death each one knows what is authoritative for him. Unfortunately we forget this when alive.
—St. Maximilian Kolbe. *Aim Higher!: Spiritual and Marian reflections of St. Maximilian Kolbe.* Prow Books / Franciscan Marytown Press.

*****

Psalm 96 celebrates God's Kingship and the manifestation of His divine glory upon the earth. The Psalm opens with the solemn proclamation: "The Lord reigns; let the earth rejoice; let the many coastlands be glad"....The psalmist describes the coming onto the world scene of the Great King who appears surrounded by a series of ministers or cosmic attendants: clouds, darkness, fire, lightning. Next to them, another series of ministers personifies His historic action: justice, law, glory. Their entrance makes all of creation tremble. The earth rejoices in all places, including islands, considered to be the most remote areas. The heavens are crossed by angelic hymns that exalt justice, that is, the work of salvation fulfilled by the Lord for the just....The advent of God's Kingdom is a source of liberation to the oppressed and joy to the upright of

heart. During this Easter season, let us celebrate with renewed hope the glorious power of God revealed in the Resurrection, His definitive judgement upon sin and death and the advent of His Kingdom of holiness, justice and peace.
—Pope John Paul II, 3 April 2002 (VIS—Vatican Information Service). With permission.

*****

Easter is a joyful season, an uplifting happiness, singing "Alleluia!", a re-awakening to the dawn of our eternal promise, the transformation made possible by Jesus Who conquered sin and death.—Alleluia! May every Sunday, indeed every day, every sunrise, every moment remind us that we are an "Easter people" called to proclaim Good News to all people and all creation, at all times, by our prayer, actions, and good works. Alleluia!

Image of the Face on the Shroud, with 3-D enhancement
formed by superimposing the positive and negative images and shifting them vertically out of alignment. Photo courtesy of Alan D. Whanger, Council for Study of the Shroud of Turin.

20

Conclusion

The Triumphant Lamb, after the Revelation of John.
Drawn by Rudolf Koch. Courtesy of Arion Press.

*****

From morning to evening, from spring to winter, all creation praises God and reminds us of Him Who is the "Alpha and the Omega, the First and the Last, the Beginning and the End" (Rev 22:13). Only in God do we find our fulfillment. As St. Augustine said, "our hearts are restless until they rest in Thee."

In biology, we learn that "ontogeny repeats phylogeny" whereby the development of the child reflects evolutionary development. Similarly, our earthly lives and our hope in the Resurrection might be considered parallel to the life of the universe, from conception in God's Mind, to expansion of the universe, development of galaxies, birth and death of stars, "restless until it rests in God" when there will be "a new Heavens and a new Earth" (Is 65:17, Rev 21:1).

Although what is visible draws our attention here, we keep our hearts, minds, and souls fixed on our God and our eternal goal, which are invisible. In the quiet of our hearts, may we grow in awareness and appreciation of the blessings of our earthly home. We thank God who made everything good. May we share life abundantly with Him. May we "go in peace to love and serve the Lord" (2 Kings 5:19, Lk 7:50).

*****

Wisdom 13: 3–5
...they should have realized that these things have a master and that he is much greater than all of them, for he is the creator of beauty, and he created them. Since people are amazed at the power of these things, and how they behave, they ought to learn from them that their maker is far more powerful. When we realize how vast and beautiful the creation is, we are learning about the Creator at the same time.

*****

St. Francis of Assisi, Patron Saint of Ecology, pray for us, that we may open our eyes to God's Presence in our world and in one another. May we be thankful for the resources we often take for granted. May all these gifts remind us to praise and thank God: sun flecks and moon-lit nights, gentle breezes and stormy winds, raindrops and snowflakes, votive candles and campfires, mountains and hills, flowers and fruits, and all creatures, praise be to God. May we be instruments of God's Peace among all the world's people and in harmony with all God's creatures. We constantly pray for a true and lasting peace.

*****

Most high, almighty, good Lord! All praise, glory, honor and exaltation are yours! To you alone do they belong, and no mere mortal dares pronounce your Name.
Praise to you, O Lord our God, for all your creatures: first, for our dear Brother Sun, who gives us the day and illumines us with his

light; fair is he, in splendor radiant, bearing your very likeness, O Lord.

For our Sister Moon, and for bright, shining stars: We praise you, O Lord.

For our Brother Wind, for fair and stormy seasons and all heaven's varied moods, by which you nourish all that you have made: We praise you, O Lord.

For our Sister Water, so useful, lowly, precious and pure: We praise you, O Lord.

For our Brother Fire, who brightens up our darkest nights: beautiful is he and eager, invincible and keen: We praise you, O Lord.

For our Mother Earth, who sustains and feeds us, producing fair fruits, many-colored flowers and herbs: We praise you, O Lord.

For those who forgive one another for love of you, and who patiently bear sickness and other trials.—Happy are they who peacefully endure; you will crown them, O Most High!—We praise you, O Lord.

For our Sister Death, the inescapable fact of life—Woe to those who die in mortal sin! Happy those she finds doing your will! From the Second Death they stand immune—: We praise you, O Lord.

All creatures, praise and glorify my Lord and give him thanks and serve him in great humility. WE PRAISE YOU, O LORD.

—Attributed to St. Francis of Assisi (1181–1226). *Canticle of Brother Sun and Sister Moon.*

*****

Lord, make me an instrument of your peace:
where there is hatred, let me sow love:
where there is injury, pardon;
where there is doubt, faith;
where there is despair, hope;
where there is darkness, light;
and where there is sadness, joy.
Divine Master, grant that I may not so much seek
to be consoled as to console,
to be understood as to understand,
to be loved as to love.
For it is in giving that we receive,

it is in pardoning that we are pardoned,
and it is in dying that we are born to eternal life.
—Attributed to St. Francis of Assisi. A well-known prayer of peace.

*****

Throughout the history of salvation and in our own lives now, God calls us and awaits our response. May our prayer, our relationship to our Creator, grow and be bountiful in the fruits of the Spirit. May we respond by devoting our whole heart, mind, souls, and strength to the love of God and neighbor, to prayer and abundant good works. May we walk with God at all times, both on the difficult Way of the Cross—and on the way to Emmaus where we finally recognize Him and rejoice with songs of "Alleluia!"

*****

Prayer is lived in the first place beginning with the realities of creation…(2569). The Psalms both nourished and expressed the prayer of the People of God gathered during the great feasts at Jerusalem and each Sabbath in the synagogues…. The Psalms arose from the communities of the Holy Land and the Diaspora, but embrace all creation. (2586).
—Excerpts from the English translation of the *Catechism of the Catholic Church* for use in the United States of America Copyright 1994, United States Catholic Conference, Inc.—Libreria Editrice Vaticana. Used with Permission.

*****

Like the praying of the Psalms during Morning Prayer of the Liturgy of the Hours, the joyful mysteries of the Rosary offer a beautiful meditation about the goodness of creation and the hope of salvation. With Mary, our Blessed Mother conceived without original sin, we pray over the happy stages of the life of Jesus. In the Annunciation, the angel Gabriel announced God's favor to Mary. As all creation has eagerly waited, in her fiat, Mary accepted God's Will for her to be the

Mother of the Savior. By her Spouse the Holy Spirit, Mary conceived God made incarnate. Mary visited her cousin Elizabeth who is with child. The child John the Baptist leapt in Elizabeth's womb. We celebrate Christmas—Mary gave birth to Jesus the Christ, the Savior, Son of God and Son of Man. Mary and Joseph presented Jesus to God in the temple. The Christ Child grew up. Mary and Joseph found Jesus teaching in the temple. All times to rejoice with Mary and the Church.

The sorrowful mysteries of the Rosary present the very sad events of Good Friday. Once again we find ourselves in a garden, but not the garden of paradise, but at the Mount of Olives. Jesus suffered agony here as He prayed about His suffering and death. He accepted the chalice of suffering. Jesus suffered terrible scourging at the hands of other men. He was crowned with thorns and thistles, beaten, and ridiculed. He carried the Cross and fell three times. He was nailed upon the Cross and died for the forgiveness of our sins. The Cross became the "tree of life" once more (Rev 22:14).

The glorious mysteries of the Rosary uplift our hope. The tomb is empty. The Shroud and wrappings are marked with the image of the Resurrected Jesus and the flowers and spices placed around His Body. Jesus is risen. Alleluia! He past through the locked doors to reassure His apostles, "peace be with you" (Jn 20:19). He gaves them a new breath of life so that they would receive the Holy Spirit. Jesus ascended into Heaven to prepare a place for us. He sent the Paraclete, the Holy Spirit, to remind us of all that He taught us. God remembered His Spouse, Mary, the Blessed Mother, upon her death, and assumed her body and soul into Heaven. Mary was crowned Queen of Heaven and now prays for us Her children, that we may love God and one another and share in God's Life now and in Heaven.

Like at Fatima, Portugal, our Blessed Mother Mary, "the Gospa", has reportedly been regularly appearing to six young people of Medjugorje since June 1981. She tells us that even the smallest flower speaks us of God our Creator's Love for us. May we "take time to smell the flowers", praise and thank God for His Love, and share that love with one another.

*****

Dear Children! Also today I call you to give glory to God the Creator in the colors of nature. He speaks to you also through the smallest flower about His beauty and the depth of love with which He has created you.
—Attributed to "Our Lady of Medjugorje", 25 August 1999.

*****

In this month's message, it concerns our developing a new relationship between our hearts and God the Creator. Mary tells us…

Also today I call you to give glory to God the Creator in the colors of nature.
All of nature speaks of God. Nature is the first step in God's revelation. God spoke and the world was created. So that which has been created is really the first proof that God exists, and that is because nothing can come about or exist by itself. The second step of revelation is the Biblical Revelation. God has spoken about Himself and about His relationship toward all of humanity and most especially toward the Israeli nation which he called "the Chosen People" from whom the Messiah was meant to come into existence. In all nature-based religions God the Creator was recognized and prayed to, and that is because every man in his heart is certain that the world and the entire Universe points toward someone who created it all. We know through history and until this very day that there always existed and still exist people who do not believe in a Creator. This means that the created world does not speak of God, but rather they declare that the world came about by itself or that material is in itself eternal. Everything that has an end must at some point also have had its beginning. And so nature speaks of God who revealed Himself in the Bible and who especially through Jesus Christ has shown Himself as our Father. And Mary wants of us to again think of this and that we may discover God in nature and then to again give Him glory.

Especially when one reads the Psalms, one often finds how the Psalmist praises the Creator and gives Him honor, and how he calls on everything that has been created to, along with him, praise and to adore God. Here let us think of Psalm 8: "O Lord, how glorious is thy name in all the earth!...who hast set thy glory above the heavens. Out of the mouths of babes and sucklings hast thou ordained strength because of thine enemies, that thou mightest still the enemy and the avenger. When I consider thy heavens, the work of thy fingers, the moon and the stars, which thou hast ordained. What is man, that thou art mindful of him? and the son of man, that thou visitest him? For thou hast made him a little lower than the angels, and hast crowned him with glory and honor. Thou madest him to have dominion over the works of thy hands; thou hast put all things under his feet: All the sheep and oxen, yea, and the beasts of the field; the fowl of the air, and the fish of the sea, and whatsoever passeth through the paths of the seas. O Lord our Lord, how glorious is thy name in all the earth!"...and of many others Psalms.

So in nature we recognize God the Creator, God the Strong One, God the Almighty One, God whose word is so almighty that it is enough that when He speaks everything is created. All of nature is in itself an absolute masterpiece, and man with all his knowledge and all his technology really creates nothing and only discovers. How touched are those scientists who became famous for discovering new laws! One of these once said: "I feel like a small boy who is playing on the beach along that huge ocean and who then finds a special little stone." Another one said: "When I succeeded at opening one door, I simply got to see 10 new doors that I knew not how to open." These are really expressions of humility in front of the secret of that which has been created. For us believers nature should really be a constant call for us to meet with God the Creator and, as it says in Holy Scripture, to give Him and only Him glory and then to pray to Him. Here we may not forget that all of nature and all of nature's laws are cooperating with God. Every growth, every move and the entire Universe and its lack of boundaries and the infinite number of stars and planets, and primarily that all of it works the way it does, is a constant miracle that should repeatedly call us to this adoration of God and to pray. Still it remains true that we first must see all this with our hearts, otherwise it can happen that although we can see everything that is happening in front us, we can still remain blind toward God the Creator. Mary, of course, wants us to discover this God the Creator and to give Him glory. Then Mary continues with…

He speaks to you also through the smallest flower about His beauty.
So we should really only accept this. When we stand before a true masterpiece and say "it is beautiful", then this remark, "it is beautiful", primarily speaks about the Master, the artist who created it. But at the same time in order to have made it, he must have first received the necessary talents—the talents of the lines or the colors that he has discovered—from God to have been able to make it and then to present it to us viewers. So no person has grounds for making himself famous or for being proud for having done something, because everything that he has, first had to come to him from God. This is a simply a grace that God gives to each one of us so that we may serve the others, but, of course, we must be grateful for all that we are able to do because again, without our free cooperation, things would also not be possible. God, who made us with our freedom, also respects our freedom.

How is one able to speak about God's beauty when St. Paul, after a vision, said: "The eye has not seen, the ear has not heard, and the heart has not hoped for what God has prepared for those who love Him"? When we think of St. Francis of Assisi or of many of the other Saints, then we can only get an inkling of what that really means what it is to feel the beauty of God with one's heart. Our visionaries, when they have spoken of their experiences with Heaven or when they just try to describe Mary, then they always say: "It is indescribable." So here we again stand before a call that all over again, I believe I may say, throws us onto our knees before God the Creator who gives us glimpses of His own infinite beauty. When a color, a flower or a fruit can be so beautiful, then how beautiful must He who created all these be!? And for this we most certainly must also be grateful in prayer and in our daily lives. It is most especially important for us to discover what Mary says next…

The depth of love with which He has created you.
...and with which He created everything. This then is certainly another step toward God, not only that nature speaks of God's beauty and His Almightiness, but about His infinite love. When God created the world, so tells us the Bible, He always said: "it is good." About man He said: "it is very good", and every one of us is for each of us a wonderful masterpiece. God gave man the strength and the possibility to cooperate with Him in the creation of life. That is why from the very beginning man was man, from the moment of conception in the mother's womb all the way to death as well as beyond death, man remains man.

What kind of secret is our physical, our psychological and our mental life really? This we will never be able to discover. So every one of us is a great secret of God's love. God wanted us, and even so if perhaps our parents did not want us or did not want a child, still God thought about each one of us! Once we have discovered this depth of love, then something really wonderful opens itself for us, and that is to be healed through God's love for us. Like it says in the Bible: "Even when a mother is able to forget her child, I will not forget you. You are written into my hand." So this love of the Father, with which He created us, should really heal us deep down in our roots of our life. This then is the reason that each of us ought to accept our life with love out of God's hand and then ought to cooperate with God in His creation.

For us Christians, who have had the special grace that this has been revealed to us, there really exists no reason at all for us to develop and carry in us inferiority complexes, or that we become jealous of someone else, or that we become greedy for something, or sad for something that we do not have that others might. God has thought about each one of us personally, has created each of us, has given us life and also all our talents. He knows and loves each of us whether we are doing well or doing badly, whether we are happy or are sad, whether we are loved by others or not, whether we are able to love the others or not, God is always here as the reason for our life, and this then also gives us the inner strength because we are afterall built on a strong foundation. God is this foundation. That is why faith and trust toward God is really what we need more than anything else in the world.

Sin is really the anti-thesis of all creation. Sin destroys, sin pulls away from the center, removes the foundation and only for this reason does man remain destroyed in the relationship toward himself, toward the others and then also toward God. That is why man, when he is in sin, remains desperately unhappy, unsatisfied, without peace, and without the ability to love. But in the depth of His love, God has also thought of this and given us by way of His Son, Jesus Christ, the opportunity to regret, that we can ask for forgiveness, and that we can then again with all trust throw ourselves into the loving lap of the Father. And when we discover God the Father's love, then he is really able to go his human way in peace, despite all his difficulties, problems and despite all his sinfulness. And this inkling of the depth of God's love will constantly give us the strength to continue with Him on the path and then one day to live eternally with God the Father, and that then is Heaven, to be in the presence of His love, constantly seeing and adoring His beauty and His Almightiness.

Here we may also mention very briefly how terrible abortion really is. There where God has given man the opportunity to cooperate in His "very good" creation, that exactly there man destroys life! Abortion is the anti-thesis of God, is an attack against God Himself, and is an attack against His love for each one of us. It is, so to say, betrayal of God the Creator that man, at some moment, says, yes to picking up his own hand and destroying what God wanted all along and kills that so wonderful life. We will only understand how terrible the sin of abortion really is as compared to how we deep we have discovered and experienced the beauty and the love in God's creation and when we find ourselves in His love with all our hearts. In other words, aborted children are only possible because we have not yet discovered and experienced God's love, beauty and Almightiness. That is why we are also able to see Mary's education. She first wants us to discover God the Creator in all that He does for us, and then we will begin to accept, love and protect our own lives and that of all others. Then Mary calls us...

Little children, may prayer flow from your hearts like fresh water from a spring.

Here Mary relies on a reality that is very easy to understand during these hot days—how important fresh water is for us. It is a condition for our lives, and so Mary wants us to go to this spring from which life flows. How can this happen? When we have been given the grace to discover the love, the Almightiness and the beauty of the Father, then it will become completely natural to pray with all our hearts, with all of our soul and in this way to seek God. And when we, for instance, love someone and know that he did something, and then begin to admire his work, then the words, the compliments and the joys are never missing. This is the way that Mary wishes us to be toward God. So when prayer becomes difficult, when we do not know what we are supposed to pray, when prayer becomes boring, or when we are distracted, it is simply because we have yet discovered God in all these dimensions. Therefore it is again so important for us to pray for the grace of discovering God the Creator. Then…

May the wheat fields speak to you about the Mercy of God toward every creature.

God's mercy is again a dimension of God's immeasurable love toward all of us, and when Mary, as she does here, wishes us to see His mercy in those everyday fruits of nature, then it is just another sign that He accepts, respects and never rejects any one of us, even when we might be rejecting ourselves, the others or even God himself. God's mercy is, only once again, immeasurable. Discovering His mercy is really healing for us because we all experience so much lack of mercy and so many wounds. And how often do we hear the questions: "How is it possible that the innocent must suffer, that there are wars, that there are people who hunger, that there are catastrophes? Where do the love and mercy of God remain?"

Certainly these questions are posed and come by themselves, but it is God's will that all people are at peace and when people are not at peace, then God wishes to turn everything to the good. God's mercy is also often praised in the Psalms and for us only one thing then remains, and that is that we, and especially so this month, discover and experience God's mercy, and then really to believe in His mercy. We must also be very careful not to project all that is merciless around us and all the wounds that we have experienced onto God Himself. God is merciful, and He will in His love someday also show His mercy to each of us. Then all this, at the end of the message should lead us again to thank and so Mary again calls us...

That is why, renew prayer of thanksgiving for everything He gives you.
Then, what is left to all people other than a "thank you"? We must therefore thank God and from this gratitude have peace, faith, hope and joy, and from the thanks toward others, then also have more of the same. This gratitude must be in our hearts and in our prayers, because this stance of gratitude is also a constant theme of Mary's. In Mary's school we wish to practice thanking every day for all that is good and to also believe that we may also thank for all the problems that we have because God will turn everything to the good.

So, let us pray...God our Father, Creator of Heaven and of earth, along with Mary, Your most humble servant, and in the name of Your Son, Jesus Christ, we wish to thank You today. Thank You for being our Father and our Creator, thank You for Your Almightiness and for Your beauty, and for Your love. But we also ask that You, O Father, open all our eyes so that may from day to day give You more and more honor and praise because You are an almighty, beautiful and loving Father. Give us the grace, O Father, that from our hearts prayer may flow like the fresh water from the spring. Open all our eyes for Your mercy and open all our hearts with the spirit of gratitude, so that we may constantly become more grateful toward You. Therefore we ask You, in the name of Your son, Jesus Christ, free us of all pride and egotism, free us of all Godlessness, from all praying to false gods, so that we may belong only to You, because You, and only You, are our God. We ask You on behalf of all those who do not yet recognize You, who do not love You, who do not hope in You and who still doubt in Your mercy, let us all discover Your love and Your Mercy, so that we all may then become witnesses to Your love, through Christ, our Lord. Amen.
—Fra Slavko Barbaric (1946–2000), Medjugorje, Bosnia-Herzec-

ogvina; 27 August 1999: **<http://www.medjugorje.org/ sb0899.htm>**. With Permission.

*****

If only everyone could see themselves, their families and communities, the environment and the entire world as God sees the world and us as a new creation precious in His Sight. May we be grateful for each person as a child of God, a temple of the Holy Spirit, then we can take better care of our neighbors. In order to have true justice and peace in this world, we have to start with our own hearts and families, then the nations can be at peace.

May we remember that we are servants of each other, and caretakers of the earth, of life and the environment, not one or the other, but both human life and the rest of creation that shares the earth with us. May we use the earth and its resources prudently, wisely, and kindly. How can we better conserve the resources we use?…We need to foster an attitude of respect for God, and all human life from the moment of conception until natural death. To gain the correct mindset to do good, we need to pray and to ask, "What would Jesus do?" In the Lenten spirit of fasting, prayer, and good works, may we better conserve water and energy, recycle, and help and teach those in need.

With human ecology founded in human solidarity, we strive to restore the land, sea, and air. May we renew the natural environment and our cities conscientiously in harmony with the natural world. We hope to protect both human lives and the life of endangered and threatened species. May God bless scientists who research the interrelationships between humankind, the flora and fauna, and their environment, and those who manage natural habitats, and our dwellings with thought for present and future generations. May pray for all people, lay and religious, teachers, doctors, nurses, and parents, that all may serve one another as Jesus. May we cooperate in justice and peace to join our efforts toward a renewed earth for now and future generations. Then with renewed enthusiasm, we can sing praise and thanks to God our Creator with all creation for His wondrous works.

*****

If you want peace, work for justice. If you want justice, defend life. If you want life, embrace truth—truth revealed by God.
—Pope John Paul II, 27 January 1999 (VIS—Vatican Information Service). With permission.

*****

Our gathering, although it is at a distance, allows us to express together the common will of safeguarding creation, to support and sustain every initiative that truly improves, cares for and preserves the earth which God gave us so that we would conserve it with wisdom and love.
—Pope John Paul II, upon signing the *Declaration on Environment* in Vienna, 10 June 2002 (VIS—Vatican Information Service). With permission.

*****

Come, Holy Spirit, fill the hearts of your faithful and kindle in them the fire of your Love. Send forth your Spirit and they shall be created, and you will renew the face of the earth. Amen.
—*Come Holy Spirit!* A well-known prayer.

About the Author

Anthony R. Brach was born in Rochester, NY. He received a B.S. in Biology from Iona College, and a M.S. and Ph.D. in Environmental and Forest Biology from the SUNY College of Environmental Science & Forestry. Anthony resides in Melrose, MA with his wife and three children.

References

Aim Higher!: Spiritual and Marian reflections of St. Maximilian Kolbe. 1994. Prow Books / Franciscan Marytown Press. Libertyville, Illinois.

Catholic Conservation Center. **<http://conservation.catholic.org/>**.

Danin, Avinoam, Alan D. Whanger, Uri Baruch, Mary Whanger. 1999. *Flora of the Shroud of Turin.* Missouri Botanical Garden Press. St. Louis, Missouri.

Good News Bible: The Bible in Today's English Version—Second Edition. 1992. American Bible Society. New York. **<http://www.americanbible.org/>**.

The Holy Bible, New international version; containing the Old Testament and the New Testament. 1978. Zondervan Bible Publishers. Grand Rapids. **<http://www.gospelcom.net/ibs/niv/>**

International Committee on English in the Liturgy. 1976. *Christian Prayer: The Liturgy of the Hours* (English translation). Catholic Book Publishing Co. New York **<http://www.universalis.com/>**.

Koch, Rudolf. 1996. *Christian Symbols.* Drawn by Rudolf Koch, with the collaboration of Fritz Kredel; translated by Kevin Ahern. Arion Press. San Francisco, California.

The Mary Foundation and St. Jude Media. **<http://www.catholicity.com/>**.

McNally, Thomas and William G. Storey. 1978. *Lord Hear Our Prayer*. Ave Maria Press. Notre Dame, Indiana.

Mother Teresa. 1983. *Words to Love By*...Ave Maria Press, Notre Dame, Indiana.

National Oceanic and Atmospheric Administration (NOAA) <**http://www.noaa.gov/**>.

Schwortz, Barrie M. *Shroud of Turin Web* <**http://www.shroud.com/**>.

Shawl, Steven and Ana. *Our Lady of Medjugorje Web* <**http://www.medjugorje.org/**>.

United States Catholic Conference, Inc. 2001. *Catechism of the Catholic Church*. 1994. Libreria Editrice Vaticana, Città del Vaticano. Urbi et Orbi Communications. Rome, Italy. <**http://www.nccbuscc.org/catechism/text/index.htm**>

Vatican Information Service <**http://www.vatican.va/news_services/press/vis/vis_en.html**>.

Walker, Winifred. 1957. *All the Plants of the Bible*. Harper. New York.

Whanger, Mary W. and Alan D. 1998. *The Shroud of Turin, an Adventure of Discovery*. Providence House Publishers. Franklin, Tennessee. <**http://www.shroudcouncil.org/**>.

Will to Love—Reflections for Daily Living by St. Maximilian Kolbe, "Prophet of the Civilization of Love." 1998. Marytown Press. Libertyville, Illinois. <**http://www.marytown.com/**>.

0-595-23707-X